to

Brice & Leigh-Marsh—

God bless you

B. Carter

John 14:2

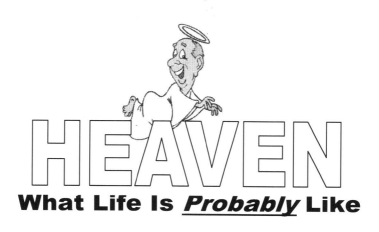

HEAVEN

What Life Is ***<u>Probably</u>*** Like

WITH A SPECIAL ADDITION OF THE INSPIRING LIFE OF SUE LENOX CURLEE AND HER MIRACLE MONDAY

By Bob Curlee

c. 2017

Jonah Publishers

Createspace

IMPORTANT NOTE- OCT 23-2017

by Bob Curlee

My wife, Sue, was killed in an automobile accident on September 20, 2017. She had a heart attack, lost control of the car and crashed into a tree. The grief is bearable because of my faith, my family and the belief that what I wrote in this book is basically true.

I decided not to try and rewrite the book.

At night when I would try to sleep, I pictured Sue in Paradise, having the time of her life with her family Plus, she loved her Alma Mater, Judson College, and she had hundreds of old classmates and friends there.

Do I miss her?

Every second of every day.

Will I see her again?

YES! You can bet your life that Jesus keeps his promises- and one day, soon and very soon, I will leave this old body; maybe float up to the ceiling; I might be led down a dark tunnel. But I will see the light, Jesus, my Lord.

Then just inside the gates of the Garden of Eden, Paradise, Sue will be waiting for me with her million dollar smile.

And that will be glory for me.

+++

*Notes on the death of Sue Curlee, and Her Miracle Monday are recorded from page 167 on to the end of the book.

*I've written a Tribute to My Wonderful Wife, Sue.
It is found on page 194.

*I thank her for the 58 years we had together-
plus I thank my Lord for going to prepare a place for her-
I thank my children for their unbelievable support
and encouragement during this time of grief-
and I thank the hundreds who prayed for me
and my family.

Bob Curlee

And God shall wipe away all tears from their eyes; and there shall be no more death, neither sorrow, nor crying, neither shall there be any more pain:
Revelation 21:4

PROLOGUE BY AUTHOR

DISMAL! BORING! DESOLATE!

My views of Heaven were rather bleak growing up. Who wants to sit around and pray all day, or listen to gloomy sermons, or sing with angels when I can't sing?

Then I was taught there is a place called Hell, and I decided I had rather than be bored than burned; I so made my reservations for Heaven through Jesus Christ.

The true Glory of Heaven is concealed from us except for a couple of Bible verses and imagery of the book of Revelation- even there it is mostly singing and praying and golden streets.

Then I wrote the book, "Secrets of the Garden of Eden," I realized our picture of the Garden is two-dimensional and is usually depicted with a chubby Adam, a plump Eve, and a lumpy Servant all eyeing a bright red apple.

I decided to dig deeper and found Adam was made in the Image of God, as was Eve. So they were neither dumpy nor lumpy- instead they were more like Mr. America and Miss Universe. My imagination began to fill in blanks and all of a sudden a Gorgeous Garden appeared, filled with flowers and trees. Eden became a place of love, joy, and peace.

When Adam and Eve disobeyed and were kicked out of the Garden, God didn't close the place down. He left Cherubim to guard it and the only "way" back in is though Jesus.

Since the word "Paradise" means "Garden," I believe that the Garden survived the Flood and was elevated up to Third Heaven, where Paul was allowed a visitors pass.

So, combining the Garden, the Thief on the Cross, the bad Lazarus's conversation with Abraham, and Paul's Unmarked Journey to Third Heaven- I arrived with the belief that saved people go to be with Jesus in that wonderful place when we die.

So join me on a trip to Heaven. I studied testimonies by dedicated Christians who had "died" and left their body. Dr. Claude Rhea floated up to the ceiling when he "died" on the operating table. Hundreds of people had experienced a dark tunnel; many have been met by a light who was Jesus; others encountered family members who had died.

Acknowledging you may not agree with all my views, I pray that you will have a better understanding of that wonderful place Jesus has gone to prepare for us.

I Corinthians 2:9-10

But as it is written,
Eye hath not seen, nor Ear heard,
neither have entered into the Heart of man,
the things which God hath prepared
for them that love him.

But God hath revealed *them* unto us by his Spirit:
for the Spirit searched all things,
yea, the deep things of God.

In the beginning God created the heavens and the earth. Genesis 1:1

HOW DID I GET UP HERE?

Good grief, how did I get up here?" I thought as I looked down on my bed and saw some old man lying there. Sue was holding my hand with her usual smile on her face but with tears in her eyes.

"He's gone," she whispered to my four children who had gathered for this special occasion.

"Nope, I'm still here! Yahoo, somehow I floated up to the ceiling," I tried to call out but no sound came from my lips. I remembered that I had been real groggy all day- probably from the medication that kept me "knocked out," but free from any pain.

"Rob, will you say a prayer for us," Sue said as she leaned over and kissed my cheek. A few tears splattered on my face- but I couldn't feel them- because I was about five feet over her head.

"Sure," my oldest son answered as he automatically reached out to take the hands of his brother and sisters. They all formed a circle around the bed holding hands as we always did for every meal or get together. Lisa was sniffing, Cathy was weeping, Jamey was shaking his head and biting his lip not to cry aloud.

Sue took my hand- or the hand of whoever was lying in that bed for it sure wasn't me. Jamey grabbed my/his/its other hand and Rob prayed, "Heavenly Father, we thank you for Dad and the many years he served you and…"

He choked up, so Jamey picked it up with his quivering voice, "So we give Him back to you, Lord. We know without a doubt He's safe in Heaven right now. Amen."

"Wait a minute," I tried to yell at them, "I'm not in Heaven- I'm just floating right up here. Look! You can see me."

I waved my hand, or I thought I did, but I couldn't see any hands or feet or any part of my body. My eyes were working quite well. I could see my family but they couldn't see me. I floated into the den and saw my grandchildren- or at least as many of them as could get there when Sue had called them that morning and told them the doctor said it could be today.

"The doctor said, 'Today,'" I thought as I wandered back through the closed door into the bedroom.

That's when it hit me.

I'm dead.

But I don't feel dead- however, I felt the greatest peace I had ever experienced. And love! As I looked at my wife- hmm, guess my widow now- Sue, I experienced that agape love I had preached all my life and thought I had experienced. Wow, it was nothing like the love I now felt for my family. It was like my heart was going to burst wide open- except I don't think I had a heart. Maybe God had let me linger a while with an invisible brain and two good eyes. It was obvious my mouth didn't function properly.

It was then I remembered those stories about people who had "died" on the operating table, hovered over their "dead" bodies and then returned to tell of all they had seen while they were "gone."

"Hey, Lord, maybe that's what you're doing with me. You are giving me a sneak preview of how Heaven will feel. In a few minutes, I'll just descend like one of those hot air balloons back into that body on the bed and shout, "Hallelujah, I have returned!! We will all rejoice and thank God for a miracle and I will get up and get out of bed…"

Who was I fooling? This was death for a Christian, or at least for some Christians. Our Father lets some of us linger a while so we can feel the real love we have for our family- the same kind He has for us, His children.

Silently I watched as each of my children went by and kissed the cheek of that man lying in the bed. Did I say, "Children?" They are all now grown, but God allowed me to have a brief slide show of each one of them. They were, without a doubt, the most beautiful kids ever created. Oops, correct that, *they gave birth* to the most beautiful grandchildren in the world.

Watching closely, I saw Jamey go to the door and inform everybody that I was gone. Gone? "Hey, I'm still here, just floating around like one of those Happy Birthday balloons."

They all put down their cell phones- which was a small miracle- looked at him and several began to cry.

Sarah, my granddaughter who is nurse, asked if she could go in and tell me, "Good-bye."

They all lined up as we always did at Thanksgiving and Christmas as if to serve their plates. There are thirteen grandchildren- and when you count grandchildren-in-laws, it stretches to seventeen. Some were not there yet, but had promised to fly in from L.A., El Paso, and Gatlinburg.

Again love swelled up inside me like an emotional tsunami! Man, I loved those kids. Sure some of them were in their thirties- and most of them out of high school- but I guess I will always think of them as "my kids." Yeah, yeah, I know they are "our kids" and had it not been for my wife, half of them would probably be in prison. But her prayers and love protected them and guided them all in the right paths.

My tear ducts were as dry as a summer pool in Death Valley, that infamous desert in California- or akin to the famous Dead Sea that I don't think Jesus ever took time to visit, Of course,

He was too busy with Living Water to worry about a deceased sea only a few miles from Jericho.

As the grandchildren trooped into the bedroom, Sue stayed sitting by my side. Every one of them hugged her- Wow, how they loved her. Once one of them had left a sign on the refrigerator that said, "I love Grandma all the time, and Pawpaw sometimes."

Of course, it was just a joke- but it was no secret that Sue was deeply loved. When we played cards, they sent a petition around the table stating that we had to let Grandma win!

Bouncing around the ceiling fan, it seemed as if I were one of those tornadoes on the ocean, called a water spout. As they suck up water, so I felt my family's love rising up to me. Normally, this would have brought me to weeping, but just as there are no tears in Heaven- undoubtedly, there are none left for those of us who depart the body and…, uh, and now what? Do I just hang in suspended animation till Jesus returns? No, Jesus told the thief on the cross that TODAY he would be with Him in Paradise. It figures then that if a thief gets instant transition, so an old preacher dead on the bed should get some kind of quick attention.

All earthly plans had already been made. We had paid for our funeral services, the casket, the grave. More importantly, I had made all my heavenly arrangements. I had served Jesus all my life- though I was not baptized until I was twelve. Then God called an awkward, skinny legged boy to preach when I was fifteen. Life had been good and relatively easy. Often I had wondered how I would react if we had lived in another country and some official would put a gun to my head and urge me to denounce my Lord. There could only be one answer, "Shoot!"

Granted, I had never made this journey through the Valley of Shadow of Death personally. But many a time, I had held hands with someone who was ready, prepared and even eager to go to Heaven.

All of this was see-sawing through my brain as I watched the proceedings below as if riding in the Goodyear Blimp. Maybe in a minute, they would all line up in front of the fireplace, tall ones on the back (and we have several way over six feet) others in front, except the small ones who knelt. Then they would make a family picture and somehow I could get a good copy of it to carry on to eternity- because as sure as shooting, I'm never going to forget a single one of them.

+++

Paradise- definition-
not just any park or garden,
but a magnificent one.
It's the same word used
in the standard Greek translation
of the Old Testament, the Septuagint,
to mean the Garden of Eden

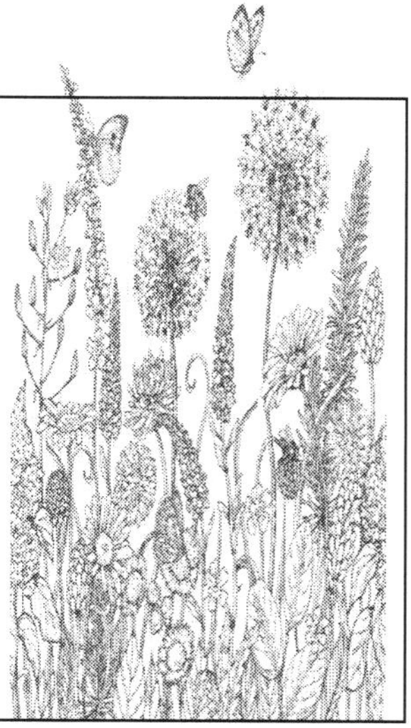

For he will command his angels concerning you
to guard you in all your ways; Psalm 91:11 NIV

MY GUARDIAN ANGEL, ROBERT-EL

Good Heavens, you scared me!" I said to someone who was now floating alongside me. Dressed all in white, it didn't take a high IQ to figure this was my angel coming for to carry me home.

It's hard to describe the real beauty of a sunset to someone who is blind or express to a deaf person a symphony, or the first smile and giggle of a new-born child.

Whoever this angel was, he radiated a splendor I had never experienced. His smile must have launched a thousand sinners to Heaven- sinners-saved-by-grace-like me.

Unaware of proper etiquette for greeting celestial beings, I went to stick out my hand- except it wasn't there. Baffled at my missing hand, I blurted out, "I'm Bob Curlee, and I guess I'm glad to meet you- but to be honest I had rather waited a few more years."

That smile beamed like a thousand spotlights as he said, "I am Robert-el, your guardian angel that has been with you all your life."

"You've been guarding me? How come I never saw you, heard you, felt you?"

"Oh, I talked with you several times, don't you remember? That night when you were fifteen at youth camp and you felt a tug and a voice telling you to go down and surrender to be a missionary?"

"That was you? But, I didn't get to be a missionary. I had asthma."

"Sure, I knew- but there was no way you would commit to being a pastor, for you grew up in a church where the Deacons always raised the dickens. You saw your dear pastor hurt time and again- so you weren't about to go forward to serve in a torture chamber."

"Right," I sighed.

"Then there was that night," the angel continued, "when things were so bad at your church you were thinking of resigning and selling funeral plots. I am the one who called out in the night, 'Don't Worry!'"

"Yeah, I remember, but it didn't work. I just kept on worrying. Hey, you were behind that trick with the light that came on and off?"

"That was neat," he smiled. "You were so bogged down with depression; one of your members had committed suicide and you felt it was your fault. You couldn't sleep so you went in the den and prayed, "Lord, send me a sign if I need to resign or stay in the ministry. Let the kitchen light shine.'"

"Ha," I laughed. "The kitchen light turned on all by itself, stayed bright for about thirty seconds, then it dimmed out."

"I thought that was a neat miracle," I said, "except I forgot to tell you whether the glowing light meant 'go' or 'stay.' Then I realized God has a sense of humor, so I went to bed and to sleep and quit worrying about it."

"There's at least one other time I whispered in your ear," said Robert-el, which by this time I had figured out was my real name. "Robert" with an "el" on the end. All the angels I knew in the Bible ended in "el," "Michael," "Gabriel," I don't remember many more."

"I can read your thoughts," my new found-friend on the ceiling said to me. "No, not all angels ended with 'el.' Do you remember one?"

"Is this some kind of quiz I have to pass to get to heaven?" I asked suspiciously.

"No- you have already made your reservations through Jesus," he chuckled. "Think hard- one of the angels, or rather, one of the cherubim, got kicked out. And his name didn't end in 'el.'"

"Lucifer!"

"Correct, when he staged war against God, our Lord booted him and millions of followers from Heaven. See if you can remember the name of another one."

"Easy- Beelzebul!"

Placing his visible arm on my invisible shoulder, I felt a brotherly love flow between us- and I knew I could trust him to get me out of this old world and safely into the next.

"Ready?" he asked.

"Uh, is there any chance I could hang around until the funeral? I would like to see who shows up."

Laughing out loud, he said, "You don't have to worry, there will be a good crowd- more than your average church attendance."

"Will Sue be all right?"

"Sure, her faith is strong- your *kids* will take care of her. Plus- Sue-el has been doing a great job protecting her."

"Sue-el? Oh, her guardian angel! So that's who bumped her and took control of the car when a tire blew and she thought she was going to wreck."

"You human beings have no idea how often we angels have to slip in and keep you from real dangers."

"Like that Christmas season when she tried to pass a truck in front of her and a car slammed into the side of her car?"

"And she walked away without a scratch," he nodded his head. "But I know you are just trying to gather a little more time down here."

"You caught me," I confessed and I noticed my arms and legs were beginning to fade back to visibility and I could see their shapes. "I just want one last look at my family, and then I'm ready to head for my just desserts."

"Ha!" my angle replied. "If you received your *just desserts you would be on the front row of H...*"

"Don't finish the sentence! I know I'm just a sinner saved by grace."

"O.K.," he nodded. "One last peek at your family and then away we go."

Suddenly I could see all of them- lined up like a Christmas picture. They were all grinning like possums. I expected one to roll out a banner that said, "Good-by, Grandpa. We will all meet you in Heaven."

Slowly they faded, except the smiles remained like the Cheshire Cat in "Alice in Wonderland," Then, Robert-el tugged on my now visible arm and we shot up through the ceiling like a space rocket.

and darkness was upon the face of the deep ." Genesis 1"2

THE DARK TUNNEL

Hey, what's happening," I yelled at my guardian angel as he drug me into a dark hole that just might end up at the county dump. *'Everything was as black as midnight down in a Cypress Swamp,'* is the way James Weldon Johnson would have phrased it. All the stories I had read about seeing a bright light ran though my head and I had labeled most of them as *Big Fat Lies.*

Whizzing through the darkness, there was a sense of motion, we were heading somewhere- but where? The blackness didn't seem to show any sign of lightening up- in fact, I could swear it was increasing. I held my one free hand up to my face- I couldn't see anything. All the while Robert-el was humming a tune that sounded like, "*I saw the light.*"

There was no light, no brightness, no glow- nothing in front of me nor behind me.

Then it appeared- a light as small as a pinhole in a dark velvet sky. My hopes arose and I felt both relief and joy at the sight of the tiny spark in the distance.

No, this was nothing like those science-fiction movies where they travel through warp space, or black holes, or just sight-seeing a new galaxy. Those tunnels consist of bright neon lights whirling past you and narrow down to a distant star.

This tunnel was black with just a tiny speck of light. But it was growing larger as we seemed to speed up to- well, who knows, but I guess it was at the speed of light!

Then it dawned on me- we were traveling into a new dimension!

"Then spoke Jesus again to them, saying, I am the light of the world:"
John 8:12

LIGHT AT THE END OF THE TUNNEL

Whoosh! It sounded like a water hose springing into action or it may have been like opening a bottle of champagne. Since this was heaven, I'm pretty sure it was more like the hose with water.

Blinking, I could not see anything- it was all too bright, like trying to watch the eclipse of the sun without the proper glasses. There was no pain- but overpowering light.

In the center a golden circle began to draw near.

It was Jesus!

He looked nothing like John's picture of Him in the Book of Revelation:

> *I turned around to see the voice that was speaking to me. And when I turned I saw seven golden lampstands, 13 and among the lampstands was someone like a son of man, dressed in a robe reaching down to his feet and with a golden sash around his chest. The hair on his head was white like wool, as white as snow, and his eyes were like blazing fire. 15 His feet were like bronze glowing in a furnace, and his voice was like the sound of rushing waters. 16 In his right hand he held seven stars, and coming out of his mouth was a sharp, double-edged sword. His face was like the sun shining in all its brilliance. Rev. 1:12-16*

Instead He looked much like his pictures we had seen since the early days of nursery at the church or in the Bible my mother read to me each night until I was old enough to read it myself.

Taller than most pictures or him, but not a giant; he was well muscled- but not like those gym freaks that have muscles like grapefruits. His face glowed- not with a halo around His head but a radiance like a street light on a foggy night. His smile would make any toothpaste company pay big bucks to have him as a model. Blue eyes sparkled as a sunny day on the Sea of Galilee. His face radiated a beauty of joy and His entire body shone like a full moon on a dark night in October.

Love radiated from him as a kid's sparkler on New Year's Eve- you could actually see it- feel it.

Falling to my knees, I felt dirty and ashamed of my backpack of sins, my lack of love and my many failures to obey him completely. I cried out, "Lord, forgive me for my many sins."

When he spoke it was a human but heavenly voice. "Don't you practice what you preached?" he said with a smile. "You told thousands of people how I died on the cross and shed my blood for the forgiveness of sins. I remember that you often would counsel some poor soul who though he was beyond redemption by telling him, *'If you confess you sins, He is faithful and just to forgive your sins and cleanse you from all unrighteousness.'"*

Breathing out a well meant, "Thank you, thank you," He reached down and took my hand. Pulling me up, He hugged me.

My body trembled, for I stood in the presence of the Lord of the Universe, yet he died on the cross for my sins.

Then with a sob of joy, I stretched my now visible arms around him and felt the warmth of his body, the beat of his heart, the deep love He felt for me.

Then He whispered into my ear, "Well done, good and faithful servant."

I wanted to shout- for that has been my goal in life- not to win awards, or have my pictures on the front of Time magazine, but just hear my Saviour compliment me as having served him well.

Then He was gone.

I suppose He had thousands of people to welcome that day.

+++

"because of the hope laid up for you in heaven "
[Colossians 1:5]

A FEW CHANGES NEEDED TO ENTER

My memory flashed back to when he was on the cross and a young punk thief cried out to him, "Lord, remember me when you come in your kingdom."

Though weary eyes, my Jesus turned and looked at him. A smile curled its way through the bloody face and a voice as if from Heaven said, "Today, you will be with me in Paradise."

My clever mind reasoned that the first person the Resurrected Christ welcomed to Paradise was that young boy- no longer in pain, no longer with tears, no longer in a ripped and torn body.

"Paradise!" Jesus said. Later Paul would call it Third Heaven. Same place.

That story rambled around in my head for a few moments, when my guardian angel said to me, "We've got to remove a few things from you and change you before you can really experience Paradise."

"Hey, I don't have anything on but this bed gown they made me wear," I said. "As you can tell, it's open in the back and I don't want to walk around Heaven with my fanny poking out."

Robert-el laughed a happy, joyful laugh, and touched my blue backless gown and instantly it changed into white clothing. Somehow I had expected a gown- and was not sure if I wanted the knee length, calf length, or drag-the-floor length. Frankly, I wasn't too hip on spending eternity in a gown anyway- for the Bible never mentions underwear for celestial beings.

White pants, white shirt, white socks and white shoes appeared on my body. I looked like Pat Boone back in his early days. Wiggling around, I was pretty sure my under garments were snow white also.

The angels at the tomb were in white as were the three *"men"* angels who appeared to Abraham then journeyed down to visit Lot. An ugly picture emerged of the perverted men of Sodom attempting to rape these same three *"men"* when they arrived at Lot's house. Apparently angels have the ability to change things for better or worse. Sodom and Gomorrah was transformed into a simmering mess: smoking ruins and a bunch of greasy spots. The whole city disappeared off the face of the earth.

"Change me?" I asked. "You mean like I just received a change of clothes?"

Again he smiled like the kid on the old Campbell Soup can. "We have to make a few changes in your memory system."

"Like taking circuit boards out of the evil Computer Hal in *Space Odyssey 2001*?"

"'Kinda' like that," he answered as he reached over and touched my head. "First, we have to remove all those sin memories that were left when Jesus forgave your sin."

"Sin memories? Like a spiritual scrapbook of my faults?"

"Maybe, but these are deep spiritual stains you carry with you after forgiveness. You call them memories, some call them nightmares. But all of those have to go for you to enjoy being here with us."

Something, or some things, in my brain gave a slight jolt as if he was unplugging the electrical cord to a computer.

Suddenly, cleanliness fell over me better than any dish washing commercial you'll ever see. Little did I know that I had been lugging around ugly memories of my mistakes, my goof-ups, my insults, my speeding tickets, all of my sins.

"Well, that didn't hurt," I said as I felt after the doctor gave me a pain shot for my kidney stones. "And I feel much, much better. Is that all?"

"No, other memories have to be removed," Robert-el said as he touched the top of my head. "You will no longer be able to remember any of the bad experiences you had on earth- the aches and pains- physical, emotional and spiritual. Your three F's have to go."

"Just a minute," I protested. "I never made an 'F' in my life- hmm- except for a paper I wrote on why white people are superior to black people."

"Really? You believed that?"

"Yeah, but thank goodness God can change people and He can change hearts," I said. "But what three 'F's' are you talking about?"

"The plagues of the earth- 'Feudin', Fussin', and Fightin.'"

It sounded strange to hear an angel delete the 'G' on the end on words- but I recalled he was my angel, so I suppose he learned my vocabulary and grammar- both good and bad.

"But I never declared war on anybody." I said.

"Really?" my angel asked. "There was never anybody you wished were dead?"

Bowing my head, I mumbled, "Well, there was a deacon or two I hoped would get run over by a truck."

"See!"

Sighing, I said, "Yeah, you need to take out all of my 'F' circuits- but I never said the F word."

"Did you ever think it?"

"On second thought, maybe I need serious surgery."

Again, Robert-el touched my head and it felt like someone just emptied my garbage can- rinsed it out- and sprayed air-freshener inside.

Cleanliness now joined with the love, joy and peace I felt.

Shaking my head around to make sure there was still a brain inside my skull, I asked, "Is that all?"

From the top of a mountain nearby I could swear I saw a cross appear for a moment and a voice as sweet as sugarcane in the summertime called down, "Father, forgive HIM for he knew not what he was doing."

A tsunami of goodness flooded my soul, but I asked my angel, "Wasn't that a misquote? On the cross didn't Jesus say, 'Forgive THEM?'"

An angelic arm wrapped around my shoulder as he said. "Don't you know that '*THEM'* is just a whole lot of *'HIMs'* and *"HERs?* Can you imagine how long it would have taken our Lord to call out each name individually?"

"Good point," I said, bouncing around happily in my newfound condition. "Hey, wait a minute! I thought there was supposed to be a welcoming committee for me- my family, my friends, a whole bunch of people I helped lead to the Lord."

Sighing, he said, "I knew there was something we forgot to remove from your old mind."

"I know, I know," I shouted. "Impatience! When the Lord gave me my basket of fruits of the Spirit, He must have left Patience out!"

"Nope. You had it all the time, you just didn't use it very much," he said as he touched my head again and it felt as if someone was having to pull out a nail that was driven in too deep.

Finally impatience came loose and so did my burning desire to hurry up and enter the gates of Heaven, or Paradise, or the Garden of Eden. I could wait.

“Am I ready, now?”

“No, we have to rid of memories of any one you know who is lost.”

“Wait a minute. Can’t I pray for my friends down there who have never been saved?”

“Afraid not. It’s too late for you- but not for them. All your remembrances of them are taken out, because there is no way anybody could be eternally happy here if they knew their son, daughter, husband, wife, drinking buddy- were not going to meet you here”

“I guess that makes sense, but…”

“There is an exception. If one of your lost souls gets saved, then you automatically know that and can recall your times together- well, all the good times- all the bad ones are not to be remembered.”

“Yeah, but what about that guy who hurt me so bad, you know, old…” I stopped because no name came forward.

Robert-el touched my face again. Shaking my heard, I asked, “Now what were we talking about?”

“Something you will never remember again.”

My brain felt so different- it felt lighter as if it has lost a few pounds- and it felt spotless like some spiritual vacuum cleaner had just done a good job on me.

There were no fears, no tears.

This type of thinking I loved- and was ready to meet other people who shared such a type of mentality- no gossip, no secrets, no dirty jokes, no put-downs.

Honestly, I had wondered if there could be any fun up here. What if they stripped out our funny bones and replaced them with praying hands?

"You don't have to worry about that," my angel said as he read my mind. "What you learned to think of as *'fun,'* has a better meaning up here- it's called *'joy.'*"

He was right- my soul felt like it was Thanksgiving Day, Christmas Day, New Year's Eve, and Valentine's Day all rolled up into one special Super Bowl- and I don't mean football.

Noticing for the first times some gates behind my angel, I said, "If those are the Pearly Gates, somebody needs to shine them up."

With that he laughed out loud. "Those aren't the doors to heaven, they are the gates to Paradise, or Third Heaven, or as it was once called, 'The Garden of Eden.'"

"The Garden of Eden? I thought it drowned during Noah's flood- killing off all the trees, flowers and the animals."

"You preachers surprise me," Robert-el shook his head. "All these years you have debated whether or not there was an ark- and if these was one, how could all the animals of the earth get on board."

"That has crossed my mind," I said.

"Quiz time," he said. "Where was the Garden of Eden located?"

"Well, nobody knows, some say it is down near the Persian Gulf; some say it was Jerusalem; and the Mormons came up with the great idea that the earth split open and it fell though and was located in Missouri."

He laughed, "I could never understand why cults emerged when God put it down so simply and so plainly all the *what's* and *where's* and *when's* and *who's*. Now He did leave out a few *'how's'"*

"Well, where was it- the Garden of Eden- or where is it?" I asked.

"The Bible tells you that it was located:

A river watering the garden flowed from Eden;
from there it was separated into four headwaters:
the Pishon, the Giho, the Tigris, and the Euphrates.
Genesis 2:10 f.

"Do you remember where that is on today's map?"

"It's either Iraq or Iran," I shrugged. "Never could tell those two apart."

"Wrong," he said. "That location is in Eastern Turkey near Mount Ararat."

"Gotcha' on that one. I can remember that archaeologists dug here, there and everywhere. But there is no evidence of Eden. So you are saying if they just take their shovels and hoes and a few bulldozers and start scratching around Mount Ararat, they will find the Garden?"

"No," he sounded a little disgusted at my lack of knowledge of geography and the Bible. "The Garden of Eden ascended into another dimension when the floods came down and the animals went into the ark."

"Ha!" I answered. "There is no way all those animals on the earth could gather there and fit into that boat. No way that polar bears and penguins and llamas could all have journeyed that far."

"I don't know how you theologians and preachers missed that one- it is so simple. Where do you think all the animals came from?"

"Africa? Asia? Europe?" I answered. "I doubt if any swam over from Australia or the Americas."

"Good grief," my angel said. "think!"

"Did they come by Flying Saucers?" I asked.

"No! No! God planted a Garden in the East of Eden. Right?"

"Yep."

"And the Garden was located in the East of Turkey?"

"Right!"

"And do you remember there is a famous mountain there?"

"Of course, Mt. Ararat! Hey, Mt. Ararat was close to the Garden."

"Right! So Noah built the ark and all the animals came from…."

"The Garden of Eden!" I shouted. "Two by two, they strolled up the gangplank and into their cages. Oops, one problem, there are still too many animals in the world to fit in that boat."

"There weren't that many," he told me as if he had a seat on the fifty yard line. "It's very difficult for you to understand, but the second chapter of Genesis refers to a special creation of man and animals. God built a Garden in the east of the land, or *eres*, or *earth,* of Eden. It's the same word where Cain goes to the land, *eres,* of Nod, to find his wife."

"There were a bunch of different earths?" I asked.

"No, there was only one heaven and earth, But the word is also used for a special territory. So the animals in the earth, eres, of Eden, left their heaven on earth Garden and marched into a smelly old boat."

"Never thought of it that way," I confessed. "So you tell me that God made the Garden of Eden near Mount Ararat, and that Adam's family stayed around close by until Noah appeared. He was told to build an ark- which I thought was big enough to hold all the people on earth- or at least in Eden- at that time. But when the population were no-shows, God allowed Noah to bring the Eden animals on board?"

"That's about it," he answered. "But there is so much more to creation than your mind can handle."

"Frankly, I don't think the scientists have done such a good job with creation," I said. "They did away with *Father God* and replaced him with *Mother Nature* and gave her a magical wand called *Evolution*."

He nodded his head and looked at his wrist as if there were a watch there- but maybe he could tell time some other way. "Hey, I've got to get you through those gates and into Paradise," he said as he tugged on my shirt sleeve.

"What about the Cherubim with those flaming swords?" I said, trying to impress him with my Biblical knowledge. "Or did their fiery swords get quenched out in the flood? Ha, ha!"

"Funny," he said. "You have spent a lifetime telling people that Jesus is the door..."

"The way, the truth and the life," I ended his sentence. "So it is through Jesus we can get past those giants cherubim and their hot torches?"

"Come on, let's try it," he led me up to the gates,

+++

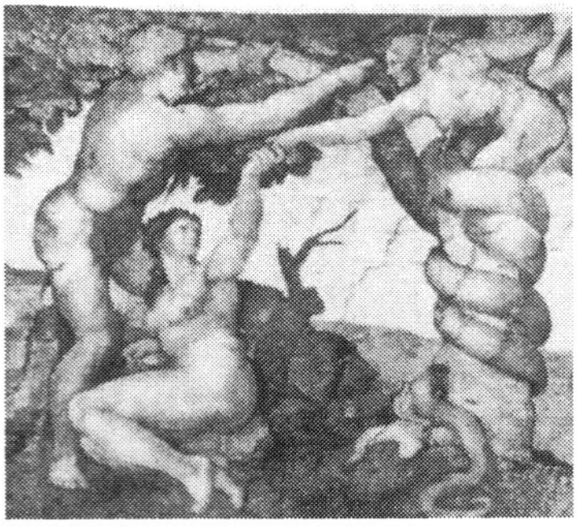

"He drove out the man, and at the east of the garden of Eden he placed the cherubim and a flaming sword that turned every way to guard the way to the tree of life." Gen.3:2-4

THE ENTRANCE TO PARADISE (THE GARDEN OF EDEN)

The Cherubim stared down at me and one of them asked in a voice like summer thunder, "What is the password?"

Fumbling through what was left of my refined mind, I turned to my angel and said, "I don't know any password, and I don't think anybody has given me one."

Smiling, Robert-el said, "Just try one."

Luckily I could still remember my password for my computer, my I-pad, Facebook, Amazon, and a dozen other things that demanded some kind of cryptic description. I knew none of them would fit- then it dawned on me. Staring the cherub right in the eyes, I said, "John 3:16."

"Close," he rumbled.

Tapping my fingers on my forehead, I thought and thought, then it hit me. Many times I had asked the congregation to stand and say three simple words- but the most important words in this world and the world to come.

"**Jesus is Lord**," I cried out at the top of my lungs.

The giant cherub actually smiled as he motioned me to enter.

Nothing on the old green earth could have prepared me for the sight that met me as I entered the Gates of Paradise.

+++

"What no eye has seen, nor ear heard,
nor the heart of man imagined,
what God has prepared for those who love him"—
1 Corinthians 2:9 (ESV),"

A LOOK AT PARADISE

Somehow I had thought Heaven, or Paradise, would be rather, well, dull. Maybe like a Sunday School class taught by an old man with a long white beard reading from the Baptist Sunday School lessons that had accumulated over the years. Of worse, I imagined Glory would be all day preaching- maybe for eternity- with us sitting on wooden benches. The redeeming factor in such ideas was that I was told early in life that there was a red hot Hell where you burned forever. So- the choice was pretty easy- get burned or get bored. I chose the boredom.

But was I ever wrong! Instead of golden streets lined with people on their faces praying, there were mountains in the distance with waterfalls. Flowers seemed to bloom and glow everywhere. A light lavender mist hung over tree tops with splashes of pale yellow and blue blending into the clouds.

+++

a treasure in the heavens that faileth not,
where no thief approacheth, neither moth corrupteth,.
For where your treasure is, there will your heart be also. Luke 12:33-34 -

THE SCENERY OF PARADISE.

Left alone by a peaceful lake that actually sang to me, I did NOT feel lonely. If fact, I felt great. A bench called out to me and I answered by taking another rest. Maybe that's why they use to put R.I.P., Rest In Peace, on gravestones. Dumb me, for years I thought it stood for RIP Van Winkle.

Gazing at the landscape before me I wondered why all the earthly pictures of the Garden of Eden are so far off mark. First, some have a hefty Eve and a plump Adam hanging around a tree with a snake dangling down. Probably most of that can be blamed on Michelangelo who painted a scene on the ceiling of Sistine Chapel making Eve looked like she would have worn about a size 18 fig leaf. Adan was no better, for he looked like Chubby Tubby. Probably plump was the in-thing back in those days. When I have time I'm going to call them up- since I am in eternity I should be able to fit most things into my schedule. Imagining them in the garden I can see a blonde Eve that would knock off all the Miss America contestants off the stage. Adam? He would be tall, dark, handsome- and muscular- not like those gym geeks that resemble thyroid trouble in their muscles.

The Garden? No artist has ever even come close to depicting it. The Bible warned us:

But as it is written,
Eye hath not seen, nor ear heard,
neither have entered into the heart of man, the things which God hath prepared for them that love him.
1 Corinthians 2:9 (KJV)

From where I was sitting it seemed as if I was back at Yosemite National Park, where there were so many waterfalls. Mark Twain said that when God finished putting all the beautiful parts in America, he had a lot left over, so He just dumped them in Yosemite.

But what stretched before me was more than a lot of mountains, rivers, and waterfalls- there was an added beauty that has never been duplicated on earth, therefore, you just can't describe it. For example, try to think of a color you have never seen. Impossible! So it is with any words that would capture the glory before me.

Artists have attempted to put on canvas what can only be experienced in the next dimension. Some painters show the Garden with floral landscapes and purple mountains majesty. Others, probably nature nuts, include all sorts of animals gathered with our great, great grandparents around a watering hole. Some show hills and rock and rills with birds of Paradise flitting back and forth.

When they made movies of the Garden, they used a couple of trees, some grass, a few flowers and not much more- except for a man and woman with their private parts carefully hidden behind bushes and Eve's hair carefully falling over her breasts. One even had a young Adam with a bit of a pot belly. Really, when God made man in His image, do you think he stuck on a roll of fat? No way.

To say Paradise is beautiful, is like saying the sky is high or the ocean is wide or Beethoven's *Ode to Joy* is cute.

There were trees- must like the original garden. They varied from tropical palms to fruit trees to golden maples in full color. Somehow I had through it would more like the Sahara desert.

There were flowers everywhere- every kind, every color.

Some were in patches, some hung from tree limbs, some lines paths that led back into the forests. All glowed.

Are there animals in Heaven? One of my church members had a dog so mean that when I went to visit her, the dog tried to chew up my tires. Finally she came out and called him off and I made it safely inside. However, I dared not step outside until she had Nero. or whatever his name was, carefully chained back up. A few months later, she came up to me before church with a tear in her eye and told me that Nero had died, did I think there was a dog heaven. Quickly I told her, that with Nero she had better hope that is not a dog hell.

Yes- just as there were animals in the Garden of Eden, there will be critters in paradise. The lamb shall lie down with the lion. Hmm, I know they will have fried chicken in heaven, but I don't know where they will keep the roosters and hens.

To my right were purple blue mountains- all with waterfalls, some with snow at the top. Snow in Heaven? I guess so, but I can absolutely assure you there's none in Hell.

To my left was a sea with sandy beaches and boats sailing gently by. Are there fishermen in Heaven? Well, yes, most of Jesus' gang loved to fish and many of my deacons would get up at ungodly hours to go fishing and brag to me about their early risings. When they would invite me to go, I would reply, "I don't care to catch them, clean them or cook them. But after they are on the table I might drop by to eat some of them.

Out in the sea there were islands that probably resembled Hawaii, or some earthly Paradise.

Behind me was a jungle, filled with trees and vines and animals. These were the same ones that roamed the original Garden of Eden- cows, horses, goats, sheep, lions, elephants, giraffes and, of course, monkeys. There were many others but I didn't feel like doing an animal census right then- when out of the trees came a little Chihuahua making a wild dash for me as if I were dog's best friend. It was *Prissy,* our little black puppy that showed up one Fourth of July and when nobody claimed her, we took her in.

Picking her up, she immediately tried to lick my face. Yuk! I put her down and said, "Go back with your critters until Sue gets here- you were her dog, not mine."

Stretching out before me were groves of trees covered in fruit that seemed to be calling out, "Come, eat me." I was a little skeptical since I remembered the terrible case of *food poisoning* that took place in the First Garden.

Woven into the orchards were dazzling displays of flowers with colors to rich you could almost eat them. Remembering my puny azaleas back home, I was awe-struck at the massive bushes that shimmered and glittered before me.

I have often wondered if the reason for flowers at funerals is to remember that first Garden- or maybe to anticipate that Paradise in the future.

Needing a little help, I called out for my guardian angel, "Robert-el."

There he was smiling and he immediately began telling me of the great time he had with the other angels. He said they loved the stories about me and my sense of humor and that they all wanted to meet me.

There's no pride in Heaven, but I did feel a bit elated as I told him to tell them to call and check with my secretary to make an appointment. That cracked him up. Man, was I glad I had an angel with a sense of humor!

"What can I do for you?" he asked. Usually he could read my mind, but to be honest there was nothing much there except the admiration of all that was around me.

"I never was very good with User's Guide Books," I confessed, "but with personal aid on the phone, I could often make a dead computer come back to life or a stubborn television leap back into action."

"What kind of help do you need?"

"Well, first, tell me about Paradise. What is it and where are we? Off in space? Or is this really a place?" I asked.

"Oh, it is definitely a Place, don't you remember that Jesus said he was going to prepare a *place* for you? There are lots of know-it-alls down on earth who argue that Heaven is just a state of mine, a nirvana, something that only exists for pink puffy souls to sleep for eternity."

I nodded then explained, "When I was young, I was pretty certain that Heaven was on the dark side of the moon- for nobody had even seen what was there. But when rockets and men flew back there- there was no a speck left of any Garden, nor was there any evidence that angels ever met there."

"I told you that we are in another dimension," he answered. "The first four dimensions space (width, depth and height) and time. God created these when He cast Lucifer out of Heaven- for the old devil had to be placed somewhere. He is eternal, but he couldn't stay in Heaven. You know that our Father is preparing an eternal place for him, his demons, and his followers."

"Yeah, I used to preach on Hell as a real place."

"Somehow in God's plan there had to be a sacrifice to bring about Justice. Some of Lucifer's followers repented, but the wages of sin is death for angels also. So God created a plan: He would make man and woman in His Image. He put them in the Garden with everything they could possibly want- but He knew that would fail, like Satan. So His plan was to one day send down His son, in the Flesh, to be the Ultimate Sacrifice for all men and angels who would ask for forgiveness and let Jesus be their Lord."

"Hmph. I knew angels sinned, especially the Cherubim, of which Lucifer was their leader. But I never thought about angels being able to repent- and what it would take to make them right with God again," I mused.

"Jesus was both God and Man, and when He died, forgive-ness was extended to all," Robert-el said.

"Did Lucifer repent?" I asked.

"Are you kidding? That puffed up, arrogant, evil being would never repent of anything. Neither would his demons."

"Sounds like a lot of folks down there on planet earth. They just can't bring themselves to admit their sins, repent, turn from their ways, trust Jesus as Lord and be saved," I added as a little sermonic note.

"Is there any special place you would like to visit?" he asked.

"Sure. I want to visit Versailles in Paris," I said. "I heard it is probably the most beautiful mansion on earth."

"O.K.," he said, "but you are going to be surprised.

We shot through the air like two anti-ballistic missiles on their way to intercept an Atomic Bomb, or a menacing Meteor, or a stray Halley's Comet. In no time flat, we stood before that great palace of Louis 14. Probably if you could Photoshop out all the surroundings, or maybe cause it to be pitch black dark and shine a spotlight on it- it would probably be impressive. Unfortunately for the building, in Paradise it looked more like an over decorated shanty in the midst of the town slums. It's not that it was ugly- it's just that Paradise is so beautiful, all earthly attractiveness is faded away in comparison.

"Why does this palace look so tacky?" I asked.

"Because it is manmade. Try thinking of some place God made that you would like to visit."

"Well, you just cancelled my hopes for a tour of the Seven Wonders of the Ancient World. I've seen Niagara Falls, how about letting me take a peek at Victoria Falls."

"Victoria Falls, next stop," he said and off we went again.

Standing on the edge of the largest waterfalls in the world, I was impressed. "I have a little knowledge of this spot, it's in southern Africa on the Zambezi River at the border between Zambia and Zimbabwe."

"Well, that's true for the time that you were on planet earth. The fact is it has been called many names- and has been surrounded by various countries and regions you couldn't pronounce."

"I can understand. I took Geography back in grammar school in the early 50's. We learned the names of the countries. When I departed to come up here, they had been named and renamed. In fact, when my son, Rob, would fly to Africa to some country of which I had never heard- I would ask Sue and she would explain where it was and what it used to me."

Gazing at the powerful surge of water, I realized that this was the Heavenly version and was even more spectacular and attractive than the one down below.

Admiring the gorgeous rainbows that glowed in the mists, I said, "So the rainbow promises us that God will never destroy his earth again by flood."

"Right, but He didn't say it would not be destroyed."

"Will you tell me exactly how the end will be?" I asked.

"I don't have a clue," he replied with a bit of twenty-first century wording. "I told you that we don't know the future- only

God knows and He will bring about the End whenever he decides."

"Will He say, '*Enough is Enough,*' before the pulls the plug?"

Again he giggled at my crazy sense of humor. "The world was made so beautiful and good. I can never understand what a mess mankind made of it."

We watched the waterfall for a little while, even diving over the edge of it, just to see what it felt like. It felt like Heaven.

Soon I confessed, "Robert-el, I felt that I would be bored to tears up here in Paradise. But in just a short while…"

"In earth time, how long do you think you have been up here?"

"Oh, I don't know. Thirty minutes? Time to call the funeral home?" I asked.

"In earth time, you have been with us for a couple of years. But up here, it's only been less than a few hour."

"So it really is true:

> *With the Lord a day is like a thousand years,*
>
> *and a thousand years are like a day.*
>
> *2 Peter 3:8"*

"Are there any people up here? I thought I would have a welcoming committee- or a least a sign-*Welcome to Paradise."*

+++

> To him that overcometh will I give to eat of the tree of life,
>
> which is in the midst of the paradise of God.
>
> Revelation 2:7

"to an inheritance that is imperishable, undefiled,
and unfading, kept in heaven for you,"
[1 Peter 1:4]

MEETING THE FAMILY

Mama and Daddy suddenly stood waiting for me. They had changed- Daddy died with dementia and a stroke, a skeleton of the man he had been. Mom had a stroke that changed her personality and she ended up in a nursing home which she called a 'Hell Hole,' and was often unhappy the last days of her life.

But now there were thirty again- dad with his shy smile and mom glimmering with love and youth. Naturally, I went to my mother first, and hugged her and hugged her, and kissed her on the cheeks and tried to tell her how much I loved her. At the same time, she was attempting to express her love for me. Then I had to go see my dad. I realized how I had never told my father that I loved him. So, in the middle of hugs, I told him over and over of the deep love I had for him- and my gratitude for raising me up right!

That could have gone on for a thousand years- and maybe in earth time it did. But I looked and saw my sister, Nelle, standing there waiting to welcome me into Heaven. Nelle had a hard life, in many ways- and yet managed to do a lot of good.

Nelle married young, had a son, Danny, then was told by her husband that he had another woman. Left to raise a child by herself, she had to move in with us. "Move-in" meant living with us in the back of a grocery store with a kitchen and two bedrooms. Fortunately Daddy was a carpenter and he built a small lean-to for my younger brother and me. Nelle had always been a little on the wild side, so Saturday nights were party-time, and Sunday mornings were sleep-ins.

That changed when I asked her to teach a Sunday School class for children at the church where I worked.

"I can't teach Sunday School and go out and party on Saturday nights," she had laughed.

"Yeah, I know."

That sunk in- deep. Tears came to her eyes and she said, "Well, I guess I'll choose to …."

I remember how my heart jumped.

"I guess I'll choose to give up my happy hours and teach Sunday School."

It was a God-thing- because at the church she met a bachelor deacon and you guessed it- they were married and raised a family of three boys- one a minister and the other two didn't miss being a preacher by much.

"Bob, honey," she said in that southern drawl that I'm glad the Lord let her keep up here. "God bless you, my little brother, for helping me get back to the Lord- and leading me to Lester."

Behind her, I saw his smiling face- just like it was when he was thirty and the two of them got married. He waved and said. "Aw-right," that same way he had when I would call him on Nelle's birthday- after she died way too soon.

Waving back, I turned and ran smack-dab into my little brother, Johnny. He combined Mr. Personality with good looks and a unique athletic ability. He had a high IQ, was one of the top ten professional putt-putters in America, played college basketball and averaged over 40 points a game in the Air Force playoffs after he entered the military.

BUT- he became an alcoholic, left his wife with four small children, and disappeared for thirty years. We had given up on him and were afraid he had been murdered and did NOT make it into Heaven.

But on my wife's 70th birthday- he called me- and like the Prodigal Son's father I went running down the road to Jackson, Mississippi, where he lived. Looking like a refugee from a garbage dump, I did not recognize him. Outwardly, he had become an old, dilapidated, worn out man- the combination of drinking, smoking and sinful living. But inwardly he had changed- into a born again Christian.

The brother who stood before me up here did not resemble the old worn out piece of a man I had met in Mississippi. Young again, he bubbled with enthusiasm and he hugged me and kept saying, "Thank you, thank you for never giving up praying for me."

Maybe we stood and talked for a hundred years, who knows, but I saw someone standing in the shadows that I didn't recognize. Black shiny hair hung around a Miss America face, with light blue eyes sparkling at me.

"You look familiar," I stammered, "but I don't remember…"

"You were only four years old," she smiled. "I'm the one you referred to in the past tense as 'little sister.'"

"Rose Marie," I said and I gave her a hug like a man who had not seen his little sister for over eighty years. "I was only four and you were three months old when you died during the night. But here you are- a beautiful woman in Paradise."

Grinning, she said, "Many people are surprised when they get here and a young man or woman comes up to them and says, 'Hi, Mom,' or 'Hello, Dad.'"

That puzzled me- then I said, "The babies who were never born- because of miscarriage or abortion! They made it here by the Grace of God."

"Right!"

"There are family reunions here that you would not believe. One dear woman had eight miscarriages and finally just gave up. Imagine her surprise when she arrived here and there were eight healthy sons and daughters waiting for her."

"What about the father?" I asked.

Bowing her head, she replied, "There is no record of the father."

"Wait a minute- every child has to have a father- and even though those children might have been sired by eight different men- they..." I stopped. Robert-el had warned me when people do not make it here, their names and records are removed from the minds of wives and children. "Oh," I said apologetically. "I remember my guardian angel had told me that all memories of lost people are removed- reminds me of an old poem:

So I wish that there were some wonderful place
Called the Land of Beginning Again,
Where all our mistakes and all our heartaches
And all of our poor selfish grief
Could be dropped like a shabby old coat at the door,
And never be put on again.

"Lolita Hiroshi wrote that beautiful poem," Rose Marie informed me. "We have a wonderful library here- full of all kinds of books."

"All kinds!" I asked in surprise.

She laughed, "I'm sure many books have probably been banned in Paradise- but the ones that made it through have been thoroughly sanitized. and pasteurized, and homogenized!"

Just to test the waters, I asked, "Do you have any, uh, I can't think of his name. The one who wrote so many books about demons and evil spirits?"

"Who?" she asked. "Do you mean Robert Louis Stephenson? His books are good, but a little dull for the new folks arriving here."

"Yeah, I imagine *'Treasure Island'* can be rather boring when you live on Paradise Island."

"This isn't an island," she informed me. In fact, it just stretches on and on, I guess, forever."

"I want to see my grandson," a feminine voice called out. Into view came a petite lady, dressed a little different from the other women.

"Grandma," I said as I rushed across to grab her in my arms, and spin her around a time or two.

The only picture I had even seen of her was when I was young, very young, dressed in something like a christening gown. Grandma Willis was a devout Methodist, so I was probably sprinkled at an early age, then baptized later.

"So, I hear you have been writing a lot of books," she smiled at me.

"Yeah, I'm writing a lot, but I think you had more readers than I did. Mom told me you wrote for the *Atlanta Journal* way back then."

"It was just little article about country life," she explained. "But I am glad your inherited my left handedness and writing skills."

"Tell me about Grandpa."

"Well, he's really your great grandfather. He's right over here. He's been wanting to meet you for a long time- you know he died years before you were born."

There stood a man dressed in a uniform that could have been for the North or the South, except it was neither blue nor gray- it was white.

"I heard you were wounded in the Battle of …" I blurted out before I realized that wars nor rumors of wars were never mentioned here. "I saw the medal you received, but I don't remember what was on it."

"Heh, heh," he chuckled. "Most of my wounds came out in the cotton fields of Georgia. It's interesting, but I hardly knew those folks in the shanties down there while I was below but up here they are my best friends. He signaled to a group of white clad people whose skin was just as pink or beige or whatever color we all were.

"Grandpa," I gasped, "those were your…."

The word "slave" never came out. Instead I felt the love that my grandfather had for those who below were treated as if they were below us. But Paradise had straightened things out- purged out the hate and prejudice and just plain meanness.

"Pa," my grandmother said, "introduce Bob to your best friend, Amos."

A friendly head bobbed toward me, and I could tell from his scars that down below he had been a … That word was not even in my memory bank.

Scars in Heaven? I never thought about that, but Jesus still bore the scars when he met Thomas a week after the Resurrection. I remembered calling Coach Bobby Bowden one day and asking him, "Coach, what would Jesus say to you if you met him today?"

That grand old Christian replied without a skip, "Well, I hope He will say, 'Well done, good and faithful servant.'"

That was clever, then I asked, "What would you say to someone who said he was Jesus?"

The response was immediate, "Show me your scars."

I rather doubt that blemish marks from my appendectomy and my three hernia surgeries made it through the gates. But maybe the martyrs and those who had suffered unjustly wore their scars here as proudly as Medals of Honor.

Amos's dark eyes sparkled and I realized he looked a lot like a young Uncle Remus. "Now don't you think these wounds on my hands and back came from your great grandfather. Not all owners were cruel, many like him were very kind and generous to us."

"Whew, that's good to hear," I said. "According to our history books, all owners were like Simon … oh foot, his last name is gone."

"Don't get me wrong, we were all glad to be free," he smiled. "All of us were proud of you when you went and preached at a Black Church during the days of segregation, and how you and our black brother Richard Cunningham would walk into Birmingham cafes and sit down, just like you were brothers."

"We were- blood brothers."

That tickled him and he pulled out a pure white handkerchief to wipe his nose. I had expected a red bandana. "Then when you went to that Centercrest Baptist Church in Birmingham, Alabama, in 1972, you opened the doors to all God's children. We even know about the bomb threats you received."

"Well, it was no big deal," I said as humbly as I could.

"Maybe it was no big deal to you, but you were the first regular Baptist Church in Birmingham to integrate. That made it easier for the others to follow."

Grandpa had to get his word in. "We even heard about that man who called you up one Monday, told you he had visited the church the day before, and chastised you for not using the King James Version of the Bible. When you told him you had black members, he mumbled and said, 'They will ruin your church.'"

Amos said, "We all applauded when you told him that he had better go on down the road and find a church that felt like he did, because you weren't changing."

Astonished, I asked, "How in the world did you know all that up here?"

"Oh, your guardian angel kept us up to date on all you did."

"All I did?" I asked hesitantly.

Again they all laughed. "No- just all the good things you did for the Lord. The things you did for yourself or the devil were left down there- far behind and out of mind."

My family and I talked and laughed together for, who knows, thirty minutes, thirty years, thirty thousand years? Time did not seem so important. Which is unusual- because I had always been a card carrying member of the fast-hash, quick-dash fraternity. Now I had patience!

+++

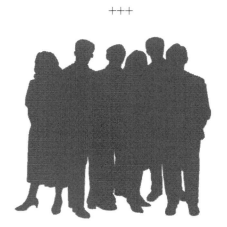

"And when he thus had spoken, he cried with a loud voice, Lazarus, come forth." John 11:43

HOW CAN I CALL LAZARUS?

Robert-el seemed pleased that I enjoyed talking with my family, but soon they all faded away like morning mists. He asked, "Is there anyone you would like to talk to?"

"You mean you have phones up here?" I asked.

"No, we have a much better way of communication and it doesn't cost you an arm and a leg."

"If it's not cell phones or internet- just how do you contact someone, say, somebody from the past?"

"How do you think?"

"Well, it's obvious landlines won't work- because this isn't really *land,* it's more like, uh, like, uh- *Heaven-lines*?"

"Close, this is Paradise, or as Paul called it, *'Third Heaven.'* You can call it Heaven if you like- but the real Heaven will only come after the return of Christ and the Judgment."

"I never could figure out all the eschatology, the return of Christ, the Rapture, the tribulation, the New Heaven and the New Earth. In fact, Since Paul made it to third heaven and returned, I often wondered what was in First and Second Heaven- say, maybe the backsliders and wayward followers?"

"I can't tell you about second Heaven, but first heaven is all of history."

"Excuse me, but did you say '*ALL* of History?'"

"Yes, it's where everything that has ever happened is recorded in chronological order."

"Everything? How in the world?"

"It can't be done in the world, but you do have an idea of First Heaven. Let me see, if I can explain. You had those video recorders down on earth, right?"

"Right! But then we added videos to cell phones and I-pads and heaven only knows what else," I answered.

"And when your granddaughter got married, someone recorded the whole ceremony, the music, the vows, the recessional, right?"

"I don't see what my granddaughter's wedding has to do with First Heaven."

"For your information, everything is recorded in First Heaven. That's true for every second or every day of every year of every century."

"I hate to sound dense, but 'How?'"

"It's kind of the way you videotaped things down there. You could record an event for things for a minute, five minutes, an hour."

"I am beginning to see the *light*. Just as man could record events down there, God has a better system that records everybody at all times. But doesn't that take a lot of tape, or digital space, or whatever??

"If there is anything God has plenty of, it's Space," he answered.

"I always wondered why he made so many galaxies when we couldn't even travel from one star to another."

"Think about it," Robert-el told me.

"Well, if space is that big that you can't see the end of it, then… Hey, I get it- then Eternity must be bigger and longer than space. Plus it shows what a Great God we have."

"Bingo," he grinned.

"But why keep records of what everybody did?"

"Judgment Day," he said.

"Wait a minute, or whatever time measurement we have up here, are you saying there is going to be a Judgment Day in the future?"

"Of course, didn't you read your Bible?"

"Yes, but, I, well, I never could figure out the when's and where's- and to make matters more complicated God added the Book of Revelation that none of us fully understand."

"That doesn't stop a lot of preachers from sermonizing on the Last Book- nor does it stop them from coming up with all kinds of weird interpretations. You will not believe how many people have *'predicted'* the date of the Second Coming- only to find themselves eating their own words, when their final day came and went."

"We had a bunch of them in my lifetime."

My guardian angel sat down on a nearby bench I could swear had not been there a minute ago. He beckoned me to be seated, and sure enough, a comfortable chair appeared.

"Let me explain a few things to you. The Old Testament, or the Old Covenant, gives all the prophecies of the first coming of the Messiah, right?"

"Right- but they are scattered hither and yon, in Psalms, Isaiah and many other books. I often wondered why if God could put the Commandments down in ten easy lessons, why didn't he just have one His writers write all the Prophecies of Jesus, in a special book of the Bible- and call it 'The Prophecies of the Messiah.'"

"Because he is a God of mystery- and just as people have to dig and hunt for precious jewels, so they have to read and pray to discover all the pronouncements of the coming of Jesus."

"So?"

"So, even though all the prophecies were there, the priests and scribes could not put them together to find a suffering servant, who being the Son of God, would die for the sins of the world."

"Yeah, they missed that one by a hundred miles," I smiled. Billy Graham was talking with a Rabbi, who told him that both Jews and Christians were waiting for the Messiah. Billy Graham laughed and said, 'Yes, but you will say 'Welcome,' and we Christians will says, 'Welcome back.'"

"Wow, we really love Billy Graham- he helped thousands and thousands of folks find their way here."

"But what about the second coming?" I asked.

"Can't you see? All of the prophecies of the return of Christ are written down in the New Testament, or to be exact, the New Covenant. You just have trouble putting them all together."

"I never was good at jig-saw puzzles, so I just preached that Jesus was coming back and you had better be ready!"

"That's good advice," he laughed.

"Do you know how and when He will return?"

"Heavens, no! Jesus said that He didn't even know when God would decide to turn out the lights, the party's over."

"But if everything is recorded in First Heaven, can't you just peek and see the when and how?"

"I told you it was all 'recorded' history. The future has not been recorded yet- which leads me to explain to you why the Final Judgment will take place in the future."

"Good, I am all ears," I said and then reached up to make sure they were still stuck on the sides of my head.

"You remember Jesus told you in the Beatitudes that if you endure persecution,

'Rejoice and be glad, because great is your reward in heaven..." Matthew 5:12 NIV)

"Yeah, and I also remember the verse:

*'Everyone who competes in the games goes into strict training. They do it to get a **crown** that will not last, but we do it to get a **crown** that will last forever. ... 1 Cor. 9:25'*

"I told Sue a hundred times, that she will have so many crowns on her head- she will have to wear a neck brace," I told him. "Maybe she will let me have a few of her Tierra's, so at least I won't look baldheaded. I heard where Queen Victoria said that when she meets Jesus, she will lay her crown down at His feet."

He smiled, "First, they are not gold crowns like you imagine, and second, Queen Victoria had the right idea. We will lay all our crowns before him."

"Okay, but I want to know when do we get our crowns, because if you notice," I said patting my head, "there's nothing up there but hair like I had back when I was thirty."

"Those will be handed out at the Day of Judgment," he said.

"You mean we are going to have to stand in line with billions and billions of people, just to get our reward?"

"It will be in a different time dimension than the one you are accustomed to. Plus, the final judging can't take place until it's all over."

"I do not understand that."

"Here's the way it works- let's take you for example. Under your preaching, hundreds came to Jesus. You helped lead all your children to Christ, and set the example for all your grandchildren. Already your sons have served in the church..."

"Yeah, my oldest one, Rob, served as children's director, youth director and music director. I told him he needed to find a church that would hire him as 'funeral director' for all the old folks."

Robert-el laughed.

The angel continued, "So all the good deeds of your children, (both physical and spiritual) and your grandchildren, and great grandchildren, etc. will bring you rewards. They can't be totaled up until the end."

"Makes sense to me," I said. "But what about those who did evil and taught their children to follow in their footsteps? Will there be great punishments for those in .... heck, what's that word?"

"Sure, but we are not going to get into that. Remember that all the folks you knew who did not make it to Heaven have been blotted out of your memory."

"Thank goodness, for there were some that I knew would bust Hell wide open!"

That tickled them both. My angel continued, "So at the Final Judgment, we will not only receive our official welcome into Seventh Heaven, but we'll receive rewards, crowns, etc. which we will then lay at the foot of Jesus. That is when He will make the final official statement, "Well done, good and faithful servant."

+++

To him that overcometh will I give to eat of the tree of life, which is in the midst of the paradise of God. Revelation 2:7 -

WHY PARADISE INSTEAD OF HEAVEN?

Back on earth I had preached that all saved people go to a place, (not a state of mind) but a PLACE called Paradise. It's going to upset those who insist of soul-sleep until the final Judgment- I don't care, let them sleep through the most gorgeous place they have ever seen.

You remember the young thief on the cross was promised to meet Jesus in Paradise- TODAY. Not tomorrow, next week, or after an asteroid wipes us out or we blow ourselves up with nuclear weapons. The scripture is pretty clear- it was on Friday afternoon, about three o'clock, that Jesus cried, "It is Finished, It is Completed," and died.

Theologians have all kinds of strange answers to where Jesus went. We know he rose from the dead, and had a chat with Mary Magdalene on Sunday morning and the disciples that night- which we call Easter.

But where was He from Friday afternoon until Sunday morning? His body was lying in the borrowed tomb- but he had an appointment with a young fellow in Paradise.

Hmm, that's complicated, and I sure don't know yet, because I haven't had time to sit down with Jesus and ask him the million or so questions I have for him.

Reading my thoughts, Robert-el startled me by asking, "Would you like to speak to the young thief?"

"Sure!"

"Good, we'll arrange that but first you might want to speak to someone else."

"Hey, I've got all eternity to talk to people from the Bible and those people who didn't make it into the Scriptures but who made it into Paradise," I replied.

"Think of somebody you might want to chat with before you meet the thief on the cross."

"Hmm, I think you are setting me up- but that's O.K., I'm pretty new at this Paradise bit."

"Put your imagination to work, you sure used it down on earth," Robert-el smiled.

"O.K., O.K., let me think. It needs to be somebody who came before the young bandit or murderer or whatever he was," I said as I scratched my head and was glad to see there is no dandruff in heaven. Come to think of it, there's really no itchy scalp either.

"How about, uh, what was that man's name that had Jesus crucified?" I asked.

"Sorry, he didn't make it here- you remember all lost people are erased from your mind."

"There were some others, but as you told me, they are nothing but blanks," I stated. "Wait a minute- or whatever you call it up here- I know who I want to talk to. Can you guess?"

My guardian angel grinned and said, "I already know, you realize I can read your thoughts."

"Well, thank God, the bad ones all got washed away by the blood of Jesus. What do you think of my choice, Lazarus?"

"Perfect- I was hoping you would choose him."

Picking through my pockets, I asked, "Well, how do I contact him? I wish you did have cell phones up here!"

"Thank goodness, we don't. The did a lot of good, but too many young Christians wasted hours on those silly things, when they could have been studying the Bible, helping people, visiting the sick. They could have even used their *brain-washing machines* to read about missionaries and Christian heroes."

"Guilty for us old folks, also. I spent a lot of time playing games- when I could have been helping folks or out witnessing,"

"All of you wasted many minutes, hours, days, even years- but Jesus forgave all your wasted time along with your sins. Let's get back to Lazarus."

"If I can't use my cell phone, Can I just make a fist into a phone and say, "

He thought that was funny and laughed in the jingle bell sound of his. Then he said, "Use your imagination, how do you think you can call Lazarus up?"

Looking around I found no phone booths, no radio stations, no television towers. Frankly, I was stumped. My family were still milling around somewhere, talking and laughing. In desperation I cupped my hands in front of my mouth and whispered, "Lazarus."

No response.

I tried it a second time a little louder- and then a third time I yelled as loud as I did at an Alabama football game.

Nothing. Nobody. It seemed as if my family had not even heard my cries.

"I give up," I said. "You will have to help me or give me an area code or an email address."

That tickled him again- of course, anything I said seemed to tickle his funny-bone, (but I was not sure angels have bones.)

"You will solve this one fast," he said. "Much faster than most folks. Think hard and remember how Jesus contacted Lazarus."

"Got it!" I grinned.

"Lazarus, come forth!"

My theory is in Paradise all people are kept on different time levels. When I *arrived,* I was on the Present Level. But I could call Lazarus up from the Time of Jesus. Later, I would learn we could also go back and visit times past. Is this Scriptural? Not really, but it does offer a method of communication and transportation up there.

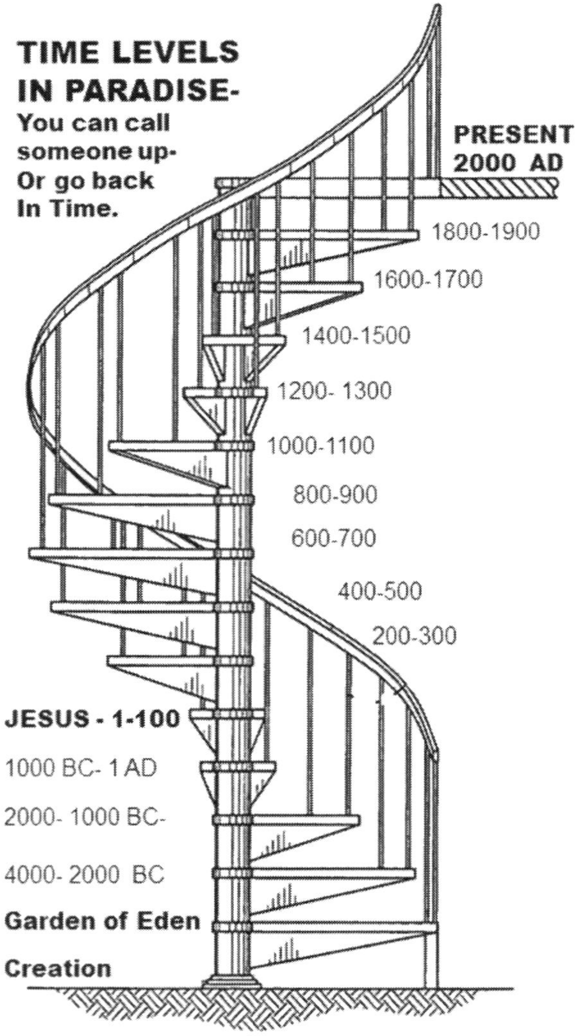

And when he thus had spoken, he cried with a loud voice, Lazarus, come forth. John 11:43

LAZARUS INTERVIEW

Instantly a handsome young man in a white robe appeared. Aquamarine eyes twinkled like sunlight on the Sea of Galilee. His smile was a sunrise and his short mustache and beard made him look like a Hollywood Star. He reached a well-muscled hand toward me and said, "It's good to meet you, Bob."

"How did you know my name?" I asked as I took his hand and shook it.

"Up here, everybody knows each other's names. It's part of our extra perks," he laughed.

Remembering my old methods of witnessing on earth, I asked, "Well, tell me about yourself. The Bible tells us very little and I want to know a lot- especially about the part where you were dead for four days- that's one day more than Jesus."

"I was never able to figure that one out," he said. "Unless Jesus wanted to prove that there is life after death."

I added, "And to prove that he was the Messiah."

"My sisters and I already knew that, it's just like all the others, we didn't really know what The Messiah meant- whether he would set up a kingdom on earth or take us all up to heaven. He wasn't very specific about the terms nor what would happen to him.

"Let me tell you my story and you can break in and ask questions any time you please," he said as he motioned us over to golden bench beneath a shady tree,

"Glad this seat is under a tree, I'll bet it would be as hot as you-know-where if it were out in the sun."

"There is no sun here, only The Son."

"I knew that," trying to cover my embarrassment. "I just imagined things get hot out in the light and God placed all these trees around to, you know, keep people from being sun-burned, or maybe SON-burned?"

Somehow he caught on to my puns and I wondered if he were speaking English, or if I were speaking Aramaic or Greek or whatever language they speak up here.

My angel nudged me and said, "It's the language that was used as Pentecost. You remember where everyone heard in their own language- it's called Heavenly Language."

"Whatever," I shrugged. "Lazarus. tell me your story."

"If I hadn't been raised from the dead," he began, "you probably would never have heard about me.

"My father raised me in luxury. I never felt the Roman whip nor experienced the poverty and hunger of those around me. Dad owned an olive press and since Bethany sits on the backside of the Mount of Olives, we had more olives than we could handle."

Pausing he looked at me and asked, "Do you know where Bethany is?"

"Sure," I grinned. "One of my deacons gave Sue and me a free trip to Israel. One of our stops was Bethany, we walked up a winding alley behind Palestinian houses- which were not very clean and the smell from dogs and their- uh- wastes was disgusting. Finally we stopped at a sign stating in English and Hebrew that this was 'The Tomb of Lazarus.' Frankly, I was disappointed for it was nothing but a hole in the ground. Well, it was a deep hole, about thirty feet. We walked down into it on slippery steps."

Lazarus laughed, "A hole in the ground! That pretty well describes what the tour guides call my grave. You have to remember that persecution by the Jews began after Jesus was killed. You recall that I was number one on their hit list. I'll tell you about that later, but now I can assure you that hole was not where I was buried and brought back to life."

He continued, "When Jerusalem fell in the year of our Lord, 70…"

"Hey, I like that," I interrupted. "'The Year of Our Lord' was placed on marriage certificates and even official documents when I was young. But by the time of my death, I think mostly Christians used 'B.C.' and 'A.D.' For years I thought A.D. meant 'After Death,' meaning Jesus death- but then I realized that there was a gap between B.C. and A.D., so someone finally clued me in on that it meant '*Anno Domini,' 'Year of the Lord.*'"

"To make matters worse," Lazarus told me, 'they didn't even come up with B.C. and A.D. until 525 by Dionysius Exiguus of Scythia Minor, but was not widely used until after 800 A.D."

"You know the atheists are trying to change it to B.C.E., Before Christian Era, and C.E., Christian Era," I added my two bits. "Say, how do you tell time up here?"

"We don't."

"What?" I asked. "How do you know when to get up, go to work, come home, eat supper, got to bed?"

"It's pretty complicated. You just know."

I popped in. "You know that body has a built-up clock- and the trying to figure out what makes it tick. There was some scientist who did a lot of research on time, but I can't remember his name.

Robert-el patted me on the back and said, “Don’t you remember that I warned you names of people who didn’t make it up here have been removed from your memory?”

“You mean that scientist, physicist, who he ever was, didn’t make it to Paradise?”

“Yep, not yet but we angels praying that he and many of the scientists will start seeing that God created the universe and mankind. Adam and Eve had built-in clock- so did Jesus.”

“This means we have an early twenty-four hour cycle, here in Paradise. This breaks down to eight for sleep, eight for work and eight to hang out with family and friends,” I said.

“’Hang out’ sounds so funny,” he giggled. The word is koinonia- it means real fellowship.”

+++

Whom have I in heaven but you?
And earth has nothing I desire besides you. Psalm 73:25

E=MC, THE THEORY OF REALITY

That scientist was a great man, but he was an atheist. He came very close to figuring out time and space when he came up with the formula, $E=MC^2$. You know what that means, don't you?" he asked me.

"I don't think anybody understands it," I shrugged. "It's the theory of relativity, which at first I figured was a formula to find who your relatives were."

Lazarus and Robert-el exploded with laughter this time. Finally my guardian angel explained, "For some reason, man has been consumed with the meaning of time- when it began, how it relates to space, and when it will end."

"So?

"It's really a shame," my angel said. "God gave that scientist one of the most brilliant minds in the world and he came so close to discovering the make-up of Heaven."

"Whoa," I said. "That man was not interested in Heaven, he wanted to prove that space and time were linked."

"True, but if he had stopped short of trying to solve all the problems of the universe with his formula, he would hit it just right. If he had left off the last number."

"E=mc? Leave off the 'squared?' I asked. "All that says is that energy equals mass times the speed of light."

"Exactly, at the Beginning- or as Scientists were so close to Creation by calling it the Big Bang- God spoke and energy erupted faster than light across the new space God has created.

At first, it was all energy, then as it slowed down, it changed to matter."

"Holy cow, you are saying that Matter is nothing but slowed down energy?"

"Not exactly, the formula reverses, 'M=e/c; Matter occurs when energy is divided by the speed of light- or when it slows down enough. All the energy changed into stars, comets, meteors, and best of all- Earth."

"Oh, in the end, it shall all turn back into Energy?"

"That's a very simple way of understanding it," Robert-el said. "Right now you need to know two things-

1- You are in another dimension.

2- Your body and all about you are made of pure energy."

"Wow, I wish I could have tapped into some of the spiritual Gatorade that last year of my life. I stayed sleepy much of the time, and hardly had enough energy to make it down to the mailbox without calling 911," I said.

Again they both snickered at my feeble attempts to understand the true nature of all God created, but then I doubt if the two knew all of it themselves.

"Hey, let's get back to Lazarus. Did time just stop for you for four days? Did Jesus came along, set the clock back those lost hours and didn't raise you from the dead? He just healed you?"

"No, no," Lazarus said. "I died and came back to life."

"Just like Jesus?" I asked.

"No, not at all. I was brought back to life, Jesus was resurrected."

"Well, pardon me, but what is the difference?

"E=mc," Lazarus answered.

"Help me, for I am beginning to see a little light at the end of that hole that is supposedly your tomb in Bethany. Jesus' mass, body, somehow reached the speed of life and he was transformed into pure energy- able to walk through walls, appear on the Emmaus Road, leap tall buildings…"

"Just back up to the first two," Lazarus said. 'Let's go back to my story and tell you all that led to my being raised from the dead."

"No E=mc; you can be D.E.A.D., then B.T.L., Back to Life?" I asked.

"Yes, but remember Jesus and I both were D.E.A.D.," he smiled. "But I came B.T.L., *Back to Life*. Jesus was *Resurrected* into a new body of energy."

"Holy smoke," I said. "What about me? Am I just a B.T.L., or have a I been Resurrected?"

"It's too hard to explain. You have not Come Back to Life from the Dead. But your body has not yet been fully Resurrected. That will happen when Jesus returns."

"I want to know what happened while you were D.E.A.D. Did you experience the out-of-body, tunnel, light, etc.?"

My angel spoke to my guest and said, "I should have warned you. He is very inquisitive."

"So was I," Lazarus said. "When I was young, I worked at the Gethsemane…"

"What, stop, you're getting ahead of me," I said. "Gethsemane is where Jesus went to pray the night he was captured."

"That was the name of a place in the grove of trees on the behind Bethany on the Mount of Olives, but it really meant, 'An olive press.'"

"Ha, we saw one of those when we were in Israel, but I think you could also use them for wine presses. I don't know if you get television up here, but I wish you could see that scene where Lucy was dancing around in a wine press. It was almost as funny as the one where she tries to wrap candy and gets behind. It was hilarious." Now I was the one laughing so hard I slapped my angel on the shoulder.

"Do we get television up here?

"Yes, but about seventy-five percent of the shows are blocked out."

"How about movies?"

"Hmm, not many. We have some 'oldies but goodies.' Books, video, movies and music are not banned up here- it's just that the bad stuff gets blocked out."

"Can they watch TV in, uh, the other place?" I asked.

Now that was funny to them. "No," they both answered.

Robert-el explained, "I have to tell you, though that music, movies, video and video games did lead a lot of people down the wrong path and led them to believe that profanity, adultery, and often, crime. If Jesus told the parable of the Prodigal Son today, he might have the wayward boy go to Las Vegas instead of a distant country."

The Prodigal Son

the water that had been turned into wine.."
and his disciples believed in him. John 2

TURNING THE WATER INTO WINE

I shook my head as so much knowledge seemed to be more than my little brain could hold. Walking over to the stream of living water flowing freely behind where we were sitting, I stooped down and took a good handful, and sipped it. 'Wow, this is good stuff! Maybe Jesus didn't turn the water to wine, he just turned it into living water."

"It was wine," Lazarus said. "I was there. It was a wedding for some of our relatives, so Mary and Martha and I journeyed up to Cana. This was our first encounter with Jesus though we had never heard of him. He seemed rather shy that night, while Peter and his disciples were guzzling down the wine and making a racket. They were mostly just smelly fishermen, you know."

"Hey, don't knock our disciples," I said.

"I'm not putting them down- I'm just being honest with you. The whole bunch was rowdy and loud. It took three years for Jesus to civilize them and turn them into Apostles," Lazarus smiled. "Let's just say that he didn't pick his followers from the upper class- he preferred to take the down and outs, and make them the up's and in's."

"I get you," I said. "Now tell me about the wedding."

"All was going well, but I don't think the father of the bride expected the Jesus gang to show up, so they ran out of wine. The host was so embarrassed; he didn't know what to do. It's like if you had the whole family over for Thanksgiving and you ran out of turkey. The hostess would probably have to run to the refrigerator and serve them bologna."

"What did Jesus do?"

"Nothing. He had not entered into the partying of his followers, in fact He sat over with his mother, just watching and taking it in."

"You watched Him?"

"I couldn't take my eyes off of him. He had the most loving expression I've ever seen on a man. As his disciples were 'the life, or death, of the party,' he never scolded them, instead he had a quiet smile on his face. Once he turned and looked at me. It was as if love shot across the room, his eyes twinkled as if to say, 'Someday we will meet again.'

"His mother, Mary, turned to Him and whispered something in his ear. I assumed it was about the wedding or the wine. I heard his remark, though it was not loud, 'My time has not yet come.'

"That made no sense to me. What time was he talking about? Time to leave, time to call his disciples down, time to take a nap? I just watched and waited.

"Then a glow came over him- I doubt if anyone noticed except Mary and me. He motioned for the servants to bring six huge empty stone water jars- each would hold from twenty to thirty gallons. They were not used for drinking but for ceremonial washing.

"Jesus told the servants in a voice that sounded kind yet full of authority. 'Fill the jars with water!' The pots were heavy and I doubt if you ever figured it up, but since a gallon of water weighs over eight pounds- and each vessel held about 25 gallons- that was over two hundred pounds. Plus the jars weighed in at about fifty pounds each- so you see, taking the pots out to the well was not an option. Instead the servants had to set up a relay line like you see with firemen, handing buckets of water from one to the other until jar number one, ran over at the top. Then the other five were filled, at the same slow pace. Half the crowd was about asleep, when they finished. Peter saw the proceedings and said, 'Water at a wedding? Craziest thing I ever heard.'

"Of course, this only irritated the host further, and he bellowed out, 'What are you dumb servants doing, filling my washing jars with more water?'

"They just pointed at Jesus and continued. Exhausted, they finally finished and turned to Mary and her son. He nodded his approval of their work and said, 'Now take some to the master of the banquet.'

"'We will be flogged for giving an ordinary cup of water to the host,' one said.

"Jesus just smiled and pointed to one of the jars of water. The servant shrugged his shoulders and reluctantly pulled out a dipper used for washing the feet of the guests. He filed it about half way and slowly made his way to the host, who looked at the dipper as if he, a Jew, were being offered a ham sandwich; finally he dared to take a sip.

"He cried out with joy to the bridegroom, 'Everyone brings out the choice wine first and then the cheaper wine after the guests have had too much to drink; but you have saved the best till now.'

"I doubt if many knew the source of the miracle," Lazarus continued. "All they cared about was more free wine. But when the disciples sat up and headed for the water- now wine- jugs, Jesus stood up and said, "That's enough. We are finished, it's time to head back to Nazareth.'

"Of course, Peter already had a cup to his lips, drank it and stared in amazement at our Lord. The others took a drink from the cup, not realizing they would drink from a cup together on the last night.

"Jesus took Mary's arm and said, 'It's time for us to go home.'

"The Bible says that this was the first of His miracles- and that at this point the disciples believed in him."

"What about the rest of the crowd? Any believers?" I asked.

"As a matter of fact, there were at least three more- my sisters, Mary and Martha, and me."

"So- turning the water into wine turned your life around," I said.

"Not around," Lazarus said. "Inside out, upside down. You see, I was rather wealthy and very arrogant. Jesus' miracle changed me. From that day on, I was a believer, and I used my wealth to help the poor, the needy. Plus, my sisters and I were able to finance much of Jesus's work."

+++

Now when Jesus saw the crowds, he went up on a mountainside and sat down. His disciples came to him, and he began to teach them. Matthew 5:1

THE SERMON ON THE MOUNT

He continued, "We went back south to Bethany, but we began to hear of other miracles Jesus was performing. Crowds followed him abound. Because of our wealth we were able to journey back to Galilee from time to time. I heard him preach the Sermon on the Mount…"

"Greatest sermon ever preached," I interrupted.

"You should have been there on that hillside overlooking the Sea of Galilee."

"Oh, I was there, on my trip to the Holy Land. I had the honor of reciting the Beatitudes to the people in our group. I dramatized it a bit, and would go to different people, place my hand on their heads and say, "Blessed are the poor in Spirit, or Meek, or Mourn, or Persecuted.'"

"How did you know that is exactly what He did with us that day? He would sit down to preach, but then he would move around and he came to Martha and Mary, placed a hand on each head and said, 'Blessed are they that mourn, for they shall be comforted.'

"Appropriate," I added.

"Not very appropriate then, for we truly lived the good life," he continued. "But when I died, they could not understand that those who mourn would be comforted- he meant I would come back to life. They thought it meant that we would all be raised at the Resurrection."

"How did they react when he told them, 'I am the Resurrection?'"

"They didn't understand. Nobody did- until it happened."

"Tell my about your death," I insisted. "I want to know if it was like mine."

"In time, I will tell you- but you need to hear the rest of the story."

"Oh, the one where the woman came and poured expensive perfume on his feet and one of the disciples- I can't remember his name- almost had a heart attack?" I asked.

Again, he laughed. "You should have been there. I had suspicions about him already. He was their treasurer but I would not have trusted him as far as I could throw him. By the way, though I can't remember his name either, did you know he was quite chubby?"

"Never thought about it," I said. "But I guess any time he was hungry he would pull up to McDonalds, or whatever you had, and order a super-sized Big Mac meal."

Giggling, he said, "You know we didn't have fast food restaurants, but we did have inns with dining rooms. And he did eat a lot. Whenever Jesus and his disciples were coming to our house for a meal, Martha would always say, 'Well, double the amount because you-know-who will be guzzling down everything."

"Ha! I never pictured him as being overweight," I said, "But what can you tell me about your life?"

"You are aware we had thieves and robbers back in those days?"

"Really?" I grinned.

"Really. Since we were wealthy, the poor guys in our hometown, Bethany, thought it was all right for them to steal from our storage houses. Often we would find where someone had dug under a wall and taken a jar of olive oil. Whoever it was never took more than one and was careful not to vandalize our storehouse. This continued until one night I went to get some more oil for our house and I caught a young man inside, with a jug in his hand. Of course, I recognized him- he was one of the pitiful young men of Bethany. I knew his mother very well. He wept and told me he was sorry- and even though I felt they were crocodile tears, I lectured him on honesty, and gave him a second chance.

"Thanking me again and again, he slipped into the darkness. I saw him on the streets of Bethany many times, for we were a rather small town. He always waved at me and smiled, and I felt that the young thief had become a good citizen."

+++

When he had said this, Jesus called in a loud voice,
"Lazarus, come forth!" John 11:43

THE DEATH OF LAZARUS

It was the next week that I felt a sharp pain in the side of my head. Martha and Mary gathered over me like two old hens and swore they would treat me and pray me back to good health.

"My vision began to blur, my speech was slurred and my right hand didn't seem to know how to write anymore. I assured Martha and Mary that it was only temporary. I had probably gotten too hot out in the olive groves.

"But I grew worse- in fact, my illness frightened my sisters so that they sent word to Jesus to come and heal me. That brightened my day and for a while, I actually felt better. Then the pain hit again, this time like a hammer inside my skull. But I knew everything would be all right when Jesus came.

"A day or two went by- but no word from Jesus.

"Finally I felt my breath being sucked out of me; I gasped, but it was too late. I died," Lazarus said, with the calmness of announcing a friend's good luck.

"You died?" I asked. "You mean you actually quit breathing, your heart stopped beating and your brain quiet functioning?"

Lazarus laughed, "We didn't know much about the brain back them, and we didn't have your machines to see if I had straight-lined; meaning I was a goner."

"I need to ask you a question, did you float out of your body?"

Lazarus gave me a quizzical look, and asked, "How did you know? If I had told anyone back then, they would have said it was a ghost or a demon inside me."

"What did you think about floating around?" I asked.

"All I knew was that the dead would be resurrected on the last day- but we didn't know what or when that would be."

"That's what Martha told Jesus, that you would rise again in the resurrection on the last day," I said.

"I could only float around close to the tomb. I did so for four days, and when Jesus finally came, my cloud like body was excited, but there was no grief for my sisters- only peace."

"Yeah, that's how I felt, but you bounced around for four days- I was out of my body only about four minutes."

Lazarus smiled, "I think I set the record for those who died and hung around for a while. I could see and hear the discussion between Martha and Jesus- and it was like an insight into the meaning of the universe when Jesus calmly told her,

> 'I am the resurrection and the life.
> Whoever believes in me, though he die,
> yet shall he live,
> and everyone who lives and believes in me
> shall never die.'

Lazarus shook his head as if remembering the greatest memory of his life. "The scribes and priests had spent years arguing about the resurrection. The Sadducees had stated that there would be no resurrection- no life after death. When you're dead, you're dead and that's it. But the Pharisees had argued that the dead would be resurrected on the last day- the day that God destroys this evil world and all the evil unbelievers."

“Didn’t they believe a Messiah would arise, defeat the enemy and then the dead would be resurrected and they would be swept up into Heaven?”

“Most of them believed that. But just as there are many *‘so-called Christian’* religions in your day they arguing over this or that. That was true with the Jews then- and now.

“’I am the Resurrection,’ Jesus said and I then realized it’s like your song,

> *‘John Brown's body lies a-moldering in the grave,*
> *His soul's marching on.’”*

“Pardon me, but I think that has to do with his purpose of freeing the slaves, rather than heading out to Heaven,” I said.

“I know what they meant in the song, but then I realized what Jesus meant in his word: He is the Resurrection- it is not a day, it is a person- and that person is Him.”

“I remember reading that Martha called for Mary- your sister. She came out pretty feisty and told him rather angrily, ‘Lord, if you had been here, my brother would not have died..”

Lazarus smiled, “I remember her falling at his feet and sobbing. Then came the second surprise of the day:

“Jesus wept.

“At first I thought he was grieving for Mary, but it hit me- Jesus was weeping for me! Me, just a nobody from a speck on a town on this world- the Lord of the Universe was crying for me. I wondered at this, until I heard someone say, ‘Look how he loved Lazarus.’”

I said, “Wow, that was some revelation- that Jesus, the King of Kings and Lord of Lords, would weep for you.”

“Oh, he wept for you, too. Remember when you had all that trouble at your church, and they… Oh, my goodness, that is blocked out of my memory.”

"Mine, too, thank the Lord," I said.

"I do know that when you were in pain, Jesus wept for you and with you."

"Wow!" I said. "I never thought of a grieving Jesus during that period- whatever it was. But I do remember He pulled a powerful miracle when He showed up at the Deacons' meeting where they had met to fire me. One man said something that set off a chain reaction and I can remember nine deacons resigned that night- instead of their getting rid of me!

I answered, "You should have heard the angels rejoicing, for it was not a victory over some human deacons, it was a victory over the Devil who wanted to hurt you, discredit you and destroy the church."

Sitting there, I was stunned to hear the heavenly account of a minor miracle that happened to me such a long time ago. Deeply inhaling the sweet, sweet scents of Heaven, and then looking over the landscape (heaven-scape), my mind thought of all those martyrs who faced wild animals. torture, and death- and how Jesus wept with each one of them. But then when they floated out of their bodies and came to The Resurrection, how beautiful heaven must have seemed to them."

"Don't you want to hear the rest of the story?" my guardian angel asked.

"Sure, sure!" I answered. "I know what happened, but I would love to hear a first-hand account."

Lazarus beamed, "Jesus wiped away the tears on his sleeve, marched up to the tomb where my body had been for four days- and where my out-of-body had been hovering around for the same amount of time. I had no idea what was coming next- I just assumed he would release me and let me go on to heaven, or Paradise, or whatever.

"Like a general in the Roman army, he commanded, 'Take away the stone!'

"Martha took him by the sleeve, trying to keep him from being embarrassed when they opened my tomb. She was sure there was nothing but a decaying, putrid body lying there, moldering in the grave.

"Jesus turned to her with that same look of absolute authority and said, 'Didn't I tell you that if you believed you would see the glory of God?'

"Mary stepped back for she had never seen this side of Jesus, with fire in his eyes. She nodded her head that he had heard his statement but I knew she didn't have a clue what it meant.

"Four or five of the husky men groaned and grunted as they pushed the stone back from my grave. Inside it was dark."

"Did it really smell like the skunk works in 'Lil Abner?"

That tickled him and he said to me, "You are something else. There is no telling what you would have said had you been there that day."

"Oh, I would have loved to have been there and experienced the great miracle Jesus performed. Didn't he just call your name and tell you to come on out?"

"That's what most people think, but if they read the Bible they would know that He lifted up his eyes and prayed,

> *'Father, I thank you that you have heard me. I knew that you always hear me, but I said this on account of the people standing around, that they may believe that you sent me.'*"

"Oops, I had forgotten that part," I confessed, "but I want to hear from you what happened next."

Jesus came to Bethany, where Lazarus lived,
whom Jesus had raised from the dead. John 12:1

LAZARUS RAISED BACK TO LIFE

I had floated back into the tomb and was hovering over my dead body when the men removed the stone. When I heard a shout that rattled the halls of Hell,

"'Lazarus, come forth.'

"Instantly I was drawn back into the dead 'me' that lay on the slab. The voice was so loud, I wondered why it didn't wake all the deceased."

I said, "I preached once that if Jesus had not called you by name, everyone would have been raised."

"Interesting idea, but not true. I was the one he called back to life- for I had been dead for four days. Immediately, I stood to my feet and walked out of the shadows into the sun light."

"Jesus smiled at me, and said,

'Unbind him, and let him go.'"

Mary and Martha did a footrace to reach me- tear away the facecloth and smother me with kisses. Bound by all the cloth, all I could do was smile and laugh. Then I looked at Jesus and he winked at me. He winked at me! That was like saying, 'We pulled a good one on them, didn't we?'"

"Jesus winked?" I asked. "I know he wept, but somehow I never saw him as one who would wink at someone."

"You didn't know him," Lazarus replied. "He would come to our home and we would swap stories until midnight. Jesus was not a emotionless person- he wept, he winked, he prayed. he praised. He could be quiet as if He were in another world, then minutes later he would be talking to us and teaching us. I never knew anyone who knew as much as He did."

"So there you stood bound hand and foot with nothing showing but your face?"

"Oh, the men quickly pulled the of clothes away- uh, except for my undergarments."

"Thank goodness," I said. "I would hate for you to have stood there unclothed- the bare facts might have come out."

"You are funny," he said. "But I believe you missed the best part of the story. Don't you remember that it states that many of the witnesses believed in Jesus?"

"Why not all of them?"

"There are always skeptics. Some shouted that it was just another trick of Jesus to make people believe He was the Messiah. Some folks won't believe the truth when they see it stuck on a stick in their face."

"But didn't you become a town hero, and win the Outstanding Citizen of the Year for Bethany?"

"Not exactly. Several rushed over the hill past the Mount of Olives and into Jerusalem and reported the event to the religious authorities."

"Did they say it was a miracle?"

"Of course not. They said Jesus was simply trying to cause an uprising of the people to follow him- and that He was dangerous. The Romans would hear of it and march into Bethany and make sure I died and stayed dead."

"So you became a target for the priests. Did they put out a poster out offering a reward for you read or alive?"

"Odd you should ask that. They did offer reward to capturing me. It was thirty pieces of silver."

"That's interesting!" I said. "Did anyone cash in on it?"

"Yes, it's not in the Bible, I was killed during the great persecution that broke out after Jesus' resurrection. Many believers were killed, but they were afraid to touch the Disciples. Finally, King Herod Antipas had James the Disciple killed. The slaughter began. My sisters were spared, but a Roman soldier rode into Bethany and slew me with a sword."

He smiled and said, "So I have able to reach Paradise before many of the Christians."

Turning to Robert-el, I said, "Wow, there was nothing on earth compared to the pleasures of being here."

For the first time I noticed that the sky was as blue as the Mediterranean, but toward the edges of the horizon, there were gorgeous sunsets. Molten gold poured over crimson clouds. Having seen the sunsets of Hawaii, I didn't think they could be outdone- but Paradise put them in the shade.

Robert-el saw me admiring the skyline and said, "You can imagine Lazarus' delight when he died the second time, and instead of a hole in the ground, he was surrounded by flower-filled valleys and the tall evergreen mountains. The waterfalls took away his breath away."

Lazarus turned as if he were leaving, and I called out, "Wait. I want to ask you about two things- the meal Jesus had at your house the day before the triumphal entry into Jerusalem that we call Palm Sunday."

Then Mary an expensive perfume; she poured it on Jesus' feet and wiped his feet with her hair. John 12:13

THE MEAL AT LAZARUS' HOME

A few days later, it was the Sabbath and *we* observed all the rules, although *Jesus picked and chose* what laws he wanted to keep. He and his gang arrived at our house shortly before sundown. They sprawled out over the couches and in the chairs in the courtyard of our spacious home. He seemed tired and quiet," Lazarus told us.

"My sister, Martha, was busy in the kitchen preparing a meal fit for a king. Mary helped- a little. I always kidded her that she would never get a husband unless she learned to cook like her sister. The twelve joined us, laughing and joking, for they were sure that soon and very soon Jesus would march into Jerusalem, throw out the dirty Romans and set up his Kingdom. James and John had already argued over who would sit at his right side.

"That man, I can't remember his name, the treasurer was elated for he would be in charge of all the money for the entire nation, maybe the world," he said. "I could never figure out why Jesus chose him. Maybe he just likes to give people a chance."

"The Bible tells us that Jesus showed up at your house later that afternoon. Martha had hurried home to prepare a meal for all of you," I said showing off my Biblical knowledge.

"Yes, Martha loved to cook and Mary loved to look. They were wonderful sisters- and you know they are both up here with me now."

"It seems like I remember Mary entered with a pint of nard, spikenard, expensive aromatic oil," I said as Lazarus smiled remembering the scene.

"Mary was a bit nervous, for this was her most expensive possession. That disciple I can't name watched with jealous eyes, wondering if she would present it to our Lord, just as the Magi had brought gifts at his birth. Was this a present for his funeral, a token of appreciation for his declaring his Kingship, or was it simple an act of love?

"You should have seen that traitor Disciple- he almost had a stroke as he leaped to his feet and screeched, 'Don't waste that expensive perfume.' Realizing he had made a fool of himself he cleared his throat and said, 'Uh, that should be sold and given to the poor.' The disciples all laughed for they knew the crook had sticky fingers and wondered why Jesus kept giving him opportunity again and again to redeem himself.

"Mary never even looked at the arrogant follower of Jesus. Frankly, I don't think she cared much for him. She opened the jar and poured it on his feet."

"He popped up again in protest. Jesus basically said, 'Be quiet, what she is doing people will remember forever- but the poor you will always have.'"

I thought for a moment and then said, "It just dawned on me that the word 'Messiah' means 'anointed one.' She was not doing this for his death as some think. But she was anointing him as the Lord who has come. Most people miss that. A lot of the do-gooders then and now criticize Jesus for accepting such an expensive gift. Of course, they also berate the church for building beautiful temples to the Lord- I suppose they forget that when God gave out the direction to Solomon for the first Temple, he didn't suggest plywood and mud bricks.

"We do not serve a cheap God. He can be found and worshipped in the lowest shack in the foulest smelling valleys- but he can also be praised on the highest hilltop, the finest of Cathedrals."

Lazarus said, "I winked at Jesus this time, for I knew that bandit wanted that money for himself. We all knew he pilfered from the pot, but we figured Jesus would handle it. Little did we know then how very ravenous that man, whatever his name, was for wealth. We would find out, however, on Thursday night, when he actually sold his soul to the devil for thirty pieces of silver."

I interrupted, "I know what happened next. Jesus's eyes must have been filled with anger as he lashed out at his betrayer."

"No, you are wrong. the Lord almost wept as he told him, 'Leave her alone. It was intended that she should save this perfume for the day of my burial. You will always have the poor among you but you will not always have me.'

"'Burial?' Martha whispered to me. 'What in the world is he talking about?'

"I shrugged my shoulders. Then I remembered hearing almost the same story where a women anointed Jesus in Bethany at the Home of Simon the Leper- who lived just down the street from us."

+++

I am he that liveth, and was dead;
and, behold, I am alive for evermore, Amen; Revelation 1:18

TRIUMPHAL ENTRY- PREPARATIONS

The second question I want to ask is about the Triumphal Entry into Jerusalem- or what we call *Palm Sunday*. Were you there?" I asked.

"Sure! Wish you could have been with me. I've seen pictures of how excited the Americans were when World War II was over, and of course, I have scenes of the great Roman victories with all their pomp and circumstance- all their parades, their crowds, their enthusiasm. But none of it compares to that day when Jesus swept into Jerusalem as the coming Messiah."

"So- you were there? I know the priests has put a hit on you because of your being raised from the dead."

"Was I there? What a crazy question. Of course, Mary, Martha and I were there. We were as excited as your University of Alabama when they win a national championship!"

"Come on now! It doesn't sound all that spectacular in the Bible."

"But it was. We gathered on the Mount of Olives, not knowing what was going to happen- but somehow God pulled a multitude of believers together. We were singing and dancing. Then the two disciples returned with the colt from Bethphage, a little town about the size of Bethany."

"Whoa! Who were those two unidentified disciples? The Bible doesn't tell us."

"Who do you think?"

"James and John?"

"Heaven's no," he laughed. "They would have fought over who would ride the colt back. You will find it hard to believe, but it was Thomas who doubted him and the one who within a week would sell Jesus for thirty pieces of silver."

"Why?"

"I don't know. Maybe he wanted to give both of them one last sense of responsibility and an insight as to his real identity."

"Hmm, well, that's interesting."

"As Jesus mounted the colt, we realized he was going to officially announce that he was the Messiah. We were certain he would march into Jerusalem- and as he turned me from death to life- he would turn the Romans from life to death. Then he would set up His kingdom.

"The crowd went wild. I even saw the young boy who had stolen wine from me in the crowd, waving a palm branch and yelling 'Hosanna.' That pleased me, for I hoped he had become a believer.

"Did you have to march around to the North Gate, because I read that the Eastern Gate was closed, except for the priests?" I asked.

"Oh, no. Jesus looked like a conquering hero as he led us down into the valley, up the road and through the Eastern Gate into the Temple area. The crowds literally went wild, as the news of Jesus swept through the city like a wildfire. When Jesus headed for the Temple, we were ecstatic.

But the enthusiasm diminished when he dismounted from the colt. He didn't run the Romans out- we didn't imagine he had come to clear the temple of the money-changers and the cheap thieves who set up booths to sell their lambs and doves- claiming they were clean. Men were shouting to buy their food while others screamed out that they had the finest wine that could be bought. It was, well, like a mob scene where every barker was trying to outdo the other.

"The money changers also thought Jesus was about to set up his Kingdom and they wanted the rights to sell their goods at His Temple."

He stopped, reflecting back on that moment. Taking a deep breath, he almost whispered. "I must confess I was caught up in the ecstasy of the crowd- and probably made a fool of myself by jumping on a table to show-off the fact that I was the first one Jesus had brought back to life.

"But at the moment two things happened almost simultaneously. Out of the corner of my eye, I saw the little thief from Bethany steal some coins from the desk of one money changer who was standing up and shouting."

"So the little thief hadn't really changed," I said. "But what was the second thing that happened.

"It was like the slow motion that you have in your movies," Lazarus said. "Jesus came down from the colt, walked over to where there were some ropes to tie the lambs. He carefully, wove them together as we watched a silence fell over the crowd. Was Jesus going to drag out the High Priest and flog him? Would he march us Tower of Antonio. the Roman Fortress that stood next to the Temple and give the general a good thrashing? We all stood and waited.

"Suddenly, he exploded and lashed out at a one-eyed money-changer who squealed and ran like a rat. Then he eyed the dozens of others who had set up shop in the Court of the Temple- he kicked over one table, threw another across the yard, and flailed out with his whip- not hitting anyone but scaring the whole bunch nearly to death. They screamed and ran for the gates. The rest of us stood there, stunned.

"Finally he stood next to the court of the lepers and loudly proclaimed, 'It is written, *My house shall be a house of prayer*, but you have made it a den of thieves.'

"The courtyard was nearly empty, because the sellers, the cattle, the sheep, the goats and even the pigeons had run for their lives and their freedom."

"What did you do?" I asked.

"We all waited in complete silence," he answered. "Having no idea what had just happened, we just stood there and held our breath for his next move. Would he walk into the Courtyard of the Priests and then into the Temple. We whispered to each other asking if he would tear down the veil of the Holy of Holies that once housed the Ark of the Covenant. We hoped and prayef he would declare Himself as the long awaited Saviour of the world.

Instead he just stood there and looked at all of us, as if in pain- as he had disappointed us.

"Where were the Temple Soldiers? Why didn't they arrest him?" I asked.

"They were all shocked by what he had done and stood frozen fearing his next move. The priests began to huddle as if they were planning a football play to stop this Jesus in his tracks.

The crowd began to cheer again and the smirking self-righteous Pharisees who had been silent yelled out, 'If you are such a great teacher, calm down your rabble rousing followers!'

"I'll bet that didn't go over too well with Jesus," I smiled.

"Of course not," Lazarus replied. "He looked them straight in the eye and said quietly, 'I tell you, if these people were silent, the very stones would cry out.'"

"Ha, I'll bet that caused them to take a look at the mighty stones on which the Temple was built and they probably speculated whether a rock could talk," I said.

"Then Jesus turned and walked back through the Eastern Gate toward the Mount of Olives. His once boisterous crowd stood stunned and silent. It was that moment the priests decided he had to die."

"And you still had no idea what kind of Messiah he would be?" I asked.

"Of course not, nobody did. Many of us were believers, but we didn't know exactly what we believed."

"You had no idea he would die on a cross that Friday?"

"No idea, at all. I don't think any of us had a clue as to what was beginning to happen."

Robert-el stood and walked over to Lazarus, put his arm around his should and said, "But you were a friend to him."

Lazarus reached over and gave me a man-sized hug, then explained. "I really must get back to Bethany. It's almost time for our meal. Martha is busy preparing the finest dinner you can imagine. And Mary, well, she is waiting to see if just perhaps Jesus will show up around supper time, as he did once before."

As Lazarus began to disappear before my eyes, I called out, "Wait. Tell me what happened to the little thief!"

But he was gone.

There was nobody around but Robert-el, so we stood and walked over to a lake where two swans swam slowly around. It was so peaceful. We found a bench and sat beneath a flowering tree that was covered with blossoms. Grinning at my angel, I asked, "Is this what the Tree of Knowledge of Good and Evil looked like?"

"Kinda'" he said. "But this one only has blooms, no fruit."

"Is there a sermon in that?" I laughed.

"Probably," he said as he stretched his arms out and placed his hands behind his neck. Inhaling a deep breath of air, he looked at me and said. “Did you ever imagine that Heaven would be this beautiful?”

“I tried to,” I answered as I gazed over the deep blue water of the placid lake. “We would visit Bellingrath Gardens near Mobile in the spring when every color azalea decorated paths and lakes and closely mowed lawns. Then when Sue and I went to Hawaii, we were sure we would see Paradise. Wow, we were surprised. The beaches were beautiful, but you had to pay to enter a garden where you can actually see the flowers. I can tell you that they don’t hold a candle to this small area that I’ve seen. It was a great surprise and pleasure to me to have a chance to meet and talk with Lazarus. May I visit him again?”

“Sure. In fact, the way it works up here, you can call someone up to where you are, or you can go back to where they are and see them in their natural surroundings.”

“Natural surroundings?” I asked.

“Wrong words,” he blushed. “I mean Paradise is constructed in time levels as I told you. Now you can go back to the time period when someone lived. You will find the same paradise gardens, but the buildings will be of that period. And their garments will look more like the ones they wore before they died.”

“I definitely want to try that- especially when I visit Adam and Eve- in the Garden.”

“Ha,” he laughed. “They will not have on clothes, but it won’t bother you any more than seeing a naked baby. This is the Garden of Eden, except larger and more splendid.”

“And the final heaven?” I asked.

“Greater than you can ever imagine,” Robert-el told me. “Of course, we can’t see it yet- until after the final judgement- when the righteous get their rewards and the thieves get their just deserts.”

"Hey, do I have time- or whatever you call it up here- to talk with one more person?"

"Certainly, who do you want to meet? Noah? Abraham? Moses? David? Peter? Paul?"

"Yes, yes, yes, to all of them," but he is the one I requested first and you had me call up Lazarus. I wasn't to talk to the thief on the cross who defended Jesus and was promised Paradise. Many have made him the Saint of Death Bed Conversions; others use him as the reason you are not saved by baptism- but by faith alone."

The angel grinned. "He doesn't have many calls, but let's see what we can do. Call him up!"

I shrugged, "I don't know how. We don't have a name for him."

"Try and see if you can figure it out," the angel said with a tease.

"Well, it's quite obvious that, 'Lazarus, come forth,' won't work. It's probably just bring him back for a repeat performance. Let's see. Hmm, No name. No address. No social security number."

"You are so funny," my angel laughed. "It's going to be a real joy whenever I'm with you."

"You mean that you are not a permanent partner to me?" I asked.

"Of course not, I'm with you now for 'temporary assistance.' Once you learn the ropes you won't need me around- but I will always come when you call me."

"Rats," I said using one of my earthly slang words. "I will miss you."

"Oh, I'll back anytime you need me. But figure out how to get to the unknown figure on the cross."

"I'll give it a try," I said. Looking around to see if there was anyone to witness my probable failed attempt, I finally said, "Thief of the cross that got saved by Jesus, come forth."

+++

"Truly, I say to you, today you will be with me in Paradise"
(Luke 23:43)

THE THIEF ON THE CROSS

Wow, I surely did not expect what happened next. Like a stroke of lightning a young man stood before me, as my grandma would say, "grinning like a possum."

I supposed I had expected some hardened, scar faced villain- but instead there was a man- a teenager- with golden curls, light blue eyes and a cream colored complexion. Before I could blurt out, 'What is your name?' he reached out his hand and said, "Hello, Bob, or maybe since you lived quite a bit longer than I did, I could call you Brother Bob. My name is Ezra, or you know me better as thief on the cross who recognized Jesus."

"Well, hello, Ezra," I said. "You don't have to call me 'Brother Bob,' it would sound strange since we all seem to be about the same age."

"Yeah," he said. "But you lived way into your eighties, and I didn't make it out of my teens."

"Why don't you two take a walk around the lake?" my angel said with a smile on his face, "I see some of my old angel buddies over there and I want to talk with them and tell them about you- they won't believe how funny you are."

Nodding to the young thief, I said, "Sounds like a good idea to me. While I was still in the flesh, in my eighties, I could hardly make it down our driveway to the mailbox and back without my back hurting and my lungs gasping for breath. But look, I can run, jump, play- just like when I was young."

I jogged on ahead on him beside the still waters of the lake, where a single swan gracefully gloated toward pink lotus blooms. It didn't take him any time to catch me, and he asked, "Do you want to race?"

"Heavens, no," I said as I pulled to a stop. "I want to talk. You may not know it but you have puzzled Bible scholars for years."

"I know," he said. "They just cannot get it in their heads that we are saved by faith- not water, not church membership, not even tithing. Hey, all of those are important, but I was saved by faith on a Friday afternoon on a cross outside Jerusalem."

"That much I know, but what led you to a cross?"

"I love the way you phrased that- 'What led me to a cross?' I was a thief, as lost as a bug in hell. I deserved the cross."

"Tell, me you story," I said, "I am all ears and mostly all mouth."

"Let me go back to before I was born- back to Bethany."

"Bethany? That's where Lazarus was from."

"I know, he is the good part of my story, unfortunately he is about the only good part. My mother was beautiful, if they had beauty contests in those days, she would have been Miss Bethany, probably Miss Judea."

"Good looking, right?" I asked.

"Too beautiful- all the men in Bethany desired to marry her, but she decided she would wait. Now here's the interesting part- guess whom she was waiting for?"

"Peter? No was married and had a mother in law. John? James? Matthew- who was probably pretty wealthy?"

"No, no, no, no, Try someone a little closer to home."

I though and then realized, "Lazarus? She was interested in Lazarus?"

"Yes, and he liked her. I think they were both young, just in their teens. So they dated, which is quite different from the present day form of dating. Mainly, it meant, Lazarus, would see her at Synagogue School, and he might drop by her house. Her father, my grandfather, was quite pleased with the arrangement and looked forward to the day they could be espoused to each other."

"Espoused? Hmm, I never realized it before, but that's probably where we get *spouse* from," I added.

"It's probably more like your engagement- but they were too young, so they had to wait, unfortunately, in the waiting, that's when the tragedy occurred."

He stopped- talking and walking. I turned around to see what had happened. "Did something happen to make you sad?"

"Oh, I can't be sad up here- but remember I can't recall bad things that happened down on planet earth. All I can remember is when my mother was about fifteen, a handsome Roman soldier had to come to Bethany, to make sure we were not planning to riot.

"Mother said he was very handsome, with blue eyes and blonde curly hair."

Suddenly, I could fill in most of the blanks, but I let him continue his story.

"At first glance, he thought he fell in love with my mother. But when he asked my grandfather about her- grandpa threw a good Jewish fit. He let the solider know that there was no way he would allow his daughter to be seen with a Gentile dog.

"As best I can tell, that did not go well with the solider. So on his next trip, he marched into their house, grabbed my mother and rode away with her- my grandparents screamed at him and begged for someone to help. Lazarus heard their cries, but realized he was just a teenager and no match for a solider.

"I cannot tell you what happened, but later that afternoon, the Roman brought my mother back home. Her clothes were torn, her hair was tangled. The solider let her down from his horse and thanked grandfather for *loaning* his daughter to him.

"From that day on, whenever the solider was coming to our town, they would hide my mother so he could not find her. He would curse and threaten to tear down their house, but he was only words.

"Finally another soldier came one week and announced he would be checking our village from now on. My family rejoiced- and nobody was any happier than my mother and Lazarus. Even though something bad had probably happened, my mother never told him anything.

"The time for the espousal was approaching, when my mother pulled grandmother aside and told her that she was afraid she was pregnant."

"'Is the father Lazarus?' she asked. 'If so, we had best get you espoused quickly, and married before the baby comes.'

"Did Lazarus know about this?" I asked, remembering the story how Joseph wanted to 'put away' Mary until Gabriel appeared.

"No, he did not," the young thief answered. "It didn't take grandmother any time to realize it had to be the blonde curly haired Roman.

"As women will do, they stuck together and as the pregnancy grew more obvious, my grandfather just assumed that Lazarus was the father. He wasn't happy, but since Lazarus was from a wealthy family he didn't complain."

"But how did Lazarus react, when he realized she 'was great with child?'" I asked.

“I don’t know,” he answered. “He must have known about the Roman soldier. But he was kind and gracious toward my mother and planned to marry her. Mary and Martha were not so understanding. In fact, they made him put off the wedding until after the baby arrived. Then he could marry my mother and adopt the child.

“When I was born, my grandmother took me from the midwife’s arms, washed the blood off my face and out of my hair. Then she gasped, for I looked back at her with blue eyes and my hair already had small blonde curls. Pushing me into my mother’s arms, she sat back and cried.

“When grandfather came, he was very proud when he was told that I was a boy- but when he saw me smile at him and blink my blue eyes, he screamed out, ‘Unclean, you have given me a grandson that is unclean.’

“Mother held me protectively, for she was honestly afraid that her father would snatch me up and carry me out into the desert to die.

“There was a tussle between all of them, until finally Grandfather settled down. He moaned, ‘There have been blue eyed Jews before, and many with blonde hair, but they were never accepted in the synagogue.’

“’We shall wait,’ Grandmother said. ‘In eight days we will carry him to the synagogue to be circumcised and the rabbi will surely help.’

“On the eighth day, my mother wore her best dress and put a pure white gown on me and carried me in a white blanket. She said I was the most beautiful baby she had ever seen.

“But that was the last of the good times in my life. The Rabbi had not seen me, though he may have heard rumors. Standing very stern, the old rabbi took me in his arms, to perform the circumcision rite. When he pulled the blanket back and saw my hair and eyes, he screeched like an owl, and practically threw me back into my mother's hands.

"'Unclean! Unclean!' he shouted over and over as he turned to a jar of water and washed his hands. 'This child cannot be a member of our synagogue, he will not be allowed to attend the Sabbath service, nor the school. He and his mother are declared outcastes. They will not be allowed to live in the same house with her parents or they too will be unclean.'

"My mother held me close to protect me, in fear that the old rabbi may stab me with the knife he used in the ritual. Instead he threw it down, spat on the ground, and left."

"What did your grandfather do?" I asked. "If the preacher had acted that way when I was baptized, my father would probably had gone up and slugged him. The same with me, if one of my grandchildren had been treated that way at baptism- I just might have gone up and tried to drown the preacher. Well, probably not, but I sure wouldn't go back to that church and listen to that preacher again."

"Grandfather was furious. His ears turned red and you could see his anger in his eyes. Escorting us out of the synagogue, he hurried down the little street to his house. Mother told me what happened there, but it's not in my memory bank, so it must have been pretty bad. We were not allowed to stay in the same house, but Grandfather built a little one room hut, next to his home. We moved there, and probably would have starved to death, but Grandmother would sneak food over to us. In the winter, when it was cold, we never knew who was the giver, but wood would appear at our front door. Maybe it was Grandfather, but I think it was Lazarus. He was devastated and would have married my mother and run off to Galilee or some foreign land. But he was young and his sisters forbade him to see my mother or the baby.

“As I grew older, none of the children in the village would play with me. They called me a ‘Gentile pig’ because my hair was curly like a pig’s tail. My grandparents never allowed us to enter their home again. Since we could not go to Synagogue, mother had learned scriptures by heart and she would recite them to me. The only people who would speak to us were the prostitutes and the lepers. But they were also unclean.

“Lazarus gave mother a job helping at the olive press and we had some money. By this time I was a teenager. Except for my mother, there no love in my heart- only hate, hate, hate. I hated my self-righteous grandparents and especially the old rabbi. In my dreams, I would march up to him, take my knife and cut off his…”

“Whoa! Whoa! Stop right there. I thought we didn’t have any bad thoughts in heaven,” I sighed.

Ezra, the young thief, looked at me, then laughed. “No, no, I was not going to cut off his … Well, let’s say I was not planning to circumcise him. I was going to cut off his beard.”

“Hey, that’s acceptable. I never wanted to chop off anyone’s beard, but to be honest, there were times when I was younger and some man would walk by with tattoos, earrings, and a pony tail- I was tempted to give him a haircut!” I confessed. “But that all changed as I grew older and found that it’s not what is on the outside of a man or woman that counts- it’s what’s on the inside. And that’s the part God looks at.”

“Of all the people who have talked with me over the hundreds of years, you are the most honest- and the craziest I have ever met,” the young thief laughed.

“Prejudice is the deep curse of mankind- whether it is Jew against Gentile, or vice versa; it can be the have’s who berate the have-not’s; or it can be the whites who dislike the blacks and the opposite when blacks don’t care for whites. Jesus came to tear all those walls down- when he talked with a Samaritan woman or helped a gentile who asked for help who said even dogs eat the crumbs from a table."

"Things were bad, huh?"

"Bad. Very bad," he said. "When I was an exiled teenager no boys would play with me and no girls would date me, I decided to get even with the world. I began to steal. Not much at first- an apple from a merchant, a coin from the tax collector's table when he was not looking. I was sly and never got caught until I broke into a storehouse that belonged to Lazarus. Helping myself to be a jug of olive oil, and some wine. I thought I had reached heaven."

He stopped and explained to me, "You wonder how I can remember those evil things about stealing. I don't know, maybe God wanted me to tell you how low I had fallen."

"Hey, as a Pastor, I've had to deal with some who were so low they could crawl under a snake's belly. I've dealt with thieves, murderers, drug addicts, alcoholics, and you name it. Some of them were saved and changed- just as you were. Others whose names I cannot remember didn't make it. Oh, I witnessed to a lot people who were not converted, but who said they loved me. I used to tell the church there was a section in hell with a banner over them, *'We love Brother Bob.'* Then I would tell them that loving me doesn't get you to heaven, it's loving Jesus."

"I discovered that while hanging on a cross," Ezra said.

"How did you become so bad, they crucified you?" I asked.

"Oh, you didn't have always to do bad things to hang on a cross. Jesus didn't. Sometimes the Romans would hang someone because they were anti-Roman, and sometimes they would crucify you just because they wanted to."

“You were telling me about stealing from Lazarus when you stopped. What happened? Did he catch you and turn you over to the authorities so they would crucify you?” I asked.

“No. Lazarus was the only good person I knew- he was a godly man and would have married my mother had she not been declared unclean. If Martha and Mary had died, instead of Lazarus, he probably would have taken me and mother with him and move somewhere to start a new life.”

“Well, what did he do to you when he caught you with a chicken in the chicken house?”

“What does that mean? he asked.

Laughing, I said, “Oh, it’s just an old saying like you were caught with your hand in the cookie jar.”

Looking puzzled, he said, “Do you mean like a wolf being caught in the sheepfold?”

“Exactly! What did he do to you?”

“Of course, he knew who I was, for you can imagine how many blonde headed boys lived in Bethany. Only one. He looked at me with my sack filled with his goods and said, ‘There is something I have always wanted to do to you.’ Then he walked closed to me and I had no idea what would happen, but he put both his arms around me and hugged me.”

There are no tears in heaven, we are promised, but there are those sweet memories that would cause us to weep. He looked me straight in the eye and said, “No man had ever hugged me before.

“To top it off Lazarus whispered, ‘Ezra, because of Jesus, I forgive you and I love you.’

“I was stunned,” he said.

“Now is this before or after Lazarus was raised from the dead?”

"Before. About a year before to be exact. I lugged my bag of stolen goods out the door, and I don't think I ever turned around to thank him. Running down the street, I entered our little house and said, 'Look what Lazarus gave us.'

"Mother smiled and said, 'Lazarus is a good man- the best man in our little village, maybe in the whole world. I have heard of a good man up in Galilee, he may be as fine as our good neighbor. His name is Jesus."

"So being caught changed your life?" I asked.

"Oh, no. There are many good men like Lazarus, but they cannot change an evil heart, and they cannot forgive the deep sins that lie there. Lazarus gave me a job, although the Rabbi was not very happy about it. Many people had slaves and he could not or did not do anything about it. By this time, I was fifteen and I figured I would steal enough money to buy passage for my mother and me. We would go to Greece or Rome. We might have to sell ourselves as slaves to someone for a while, but eventually we would be free.

"It was then that Lazarus died. News of his sickness spread through Bethany and many had prayed for him. I did not pray. I did not have any God to whom I could pray. Soon we learned that his sisters had sent to Jesus to come and heal their brother. That was good news, because Lazarus was good to us.

"But Jesus did not come. Lazarus died, and my heart sunk. He was the only person besides Mother I had ever cared for.

"I wept.

"For the first time in my life, I cried. Life spiraled down until I heard a great commotion that this Jesus had come to town. Naturally, I wanted to see this great man who had healed the sick, walked on water, fed the thousands. So I was there just to see what happened.

"Mary was with him. Martha rushed out and I thought she was going to give him a piece of her mind. But she was calm. I heard them say something about 'Resurrection,' but I didn't believe in it. If it were true, as evil as I had been, I would surely end up in the fires of Hell.

"Finally Jesus went up toward the cave where they had buried him. He said some kind of prayer, then he yelled out with a voice like thunder, 'Lazarus, come forth.'

"Sitting in a tree, I almost fell out, when this mummy figure walked out of the grave. I didn't know who it was. But they took away the head cloth- and it was Lazarus. I was so excited, I started shouting. The crowd picked it up and they cheered and rejoiced as Lazarus came back to life.

"I wondered who was this man, Jesus? As he looked around the crowd, he saw me. He had blue eyes! They were the kindest, most gentle eyes I have ever seen. He smiled at me as if to say, 'I want to meet you someday.'

"Mary and Martha insisted Jesus hurry to their home- where they would prepare a great feast and invite all of Bethany. That is, all of Bethany except Mother and me."

"Did you become a believer then?" I asked.

"No. I was too much a rebel to give my heart to someone just because he raised someone from the grave. My mother and I were waiting for the real Messiah. He would kill off all the Roman soldiers, especially one blued eye man with blonde curly hair. I would join the army and be part of his kingdom- when the real Messiah came."

"Did you see Lazarus again?" I asked.

"Not until Sunday. On the Sabbath we heard that Jesus was back in town and had supper with Mary and her family."

"What happened Sunday?" I asked.

Laughing he said, "You are playing with me. You know exactly what happened that day. Some special force of energy was in the air that morning. Getting up early, I felt the need to hike over the Mount of Olives. So grabbing a hard roll for breakfast, I heard a lot of commotion as the town headed out toward the road to the olive groves. Taking the shortcut through the trees I thought I would be the first there, but when I arrived there was already a crowd of people shaking with expectation. Nobody recognized me, but I put a shawl over my head and ventured into the multitude to find out what was happening.

"Then Jesus appeared with the throng from my home town. Keeping my head low, I stayed out on the edges. Something great was about to happen. The Messiah had arrived. The Kingdom of Rome was going to begin and The Lord Messiah would reign forever. Then I realized we were going to march into Jerusalem- and I would be part of it. That was the happiest day of my miserable life.

"I wondered why Jesus was riding on a donkey instead of a great white horse. Several older men around me chuckled, that this was the fulfillment for the Messiah- to enter Jerusalem on a colt or a donkey.

"Some girl came by handing out palm leaves, I took one as she looked at me strangely, My hair was hidden, but my blue eyes were obvious. Looking up at Jesus with his sky-blue eyes, she nodded her head as if she understood not all Jews had dark eyes. Waving my palm branch and hollering, 'Hosanna' as loud as I could- we marched down the road and I thought we would turn and head to the north gate. Everyone knew the Eastern Gate was closed to all except a few rabbis when they had a special meeting.

"I had been to Jerusalem many times to look for things to steal- and was usually quite lucky. Crowds were so thick up the main street, it was easy to pick a man's purse, or slip a chicken from one of the many booths there.

"But today, stealing was not on my mind. I had seen the Messiah- and he had seen me. Now I was part of his group marching up the road and in through the Eastern Gate.

"The temple was always breath-taking. It's white marble and gold trim were the most beautiful sights in the world to me. Jesus led and we went marching and yelling all the way past the court of the Gentiles and into the Court of the Women. This was my first time there. As an unclean Jew, I could only wander around in the outer courts.

"Crowds inside the gates joined our festivity- the Messiah had arrived. There was dancing and singing and weeping and laughing all merged into one huge crescendo," he told me dreamily as if he were back there once again.

"Well, I know what the Bible says and what Lazarus told me, but you were also a witness to what happened next," I said. "What is your version of what took place?"

"Jesus stopped and stepped down from the donkey. Around him groups of people were pressing forward to watch him overthrow the dreadful Romans. There was a blonde Roman soldier I hoped I would find and plunge a sword into his chest."

I gasped, and he said, "You know, I wasn't a Christian at the point. My evil mind was still at work. Then it happened, an earthquake shook my dream world as Jesus took a whip of cords- and headed toward the money changers- instead of the Temple. With a grunt, he threw over a table and money scattered everywhere. This pleased the crowd, until he began to kick over tables where people sold their sacrifices for the altar.

"Then, just as quick as a storm passes over, he stopped, looked around and said something about God's house shall be a house of prayer for all nations.

“The merchants and moneychangers were trying to gather up their wares or chase down their animals- but the crowd yelled in support of him. That is, they yelled, until he turned and walked back out of the courts of the temple, back through the Eastern Gate, back toward the Mount of Olives and back to Bethany.

“He’s a fake,” I thought. “The Messiah was to set up a new kingdom on this earth- and this Jesus person only rattled a few greedy traders. Disgusted and disappointed, I did what my old natural self would do. Quickly I scrambled to the floor and started picking up coins. I was doing very well with my stealing until I bumped into the legs of a Temple guard.

“’You are a thief,’ he growled as he snatched me up and drug me toward the gates.

“No. No. You don’t understand,” I pleaded as my sinful mind jumped into action. “I am the son of one of the money changers and I was only helping my father retrieve what he had lost.

“Jerking off my headpiece, he saw my blonde hair and said, ‘I know who you are, that little unclean bastard from Bethany. You are nothing but a thief and you are going to pay for what you have done.’

“I was tried and found guilty- and I thought they would just be placed me a dark, dismal Roman prison for a few days. But instead, I ended up nailed to a cross on that Black Friday. All hope was lost. I had no hope of heaven for I was not a good Jew- and I had heard of the fires of hell.

“Shivering, quivering, on the cross on the chilly April afternoon, I was in much pain and groaned constantly.

“On a cross nearby hung a wicked old man who spewed out profanity to the guards and to the crowd and even God. I yelled at the old murderer to shut up, but he sneered at me and only screeched louder.”

"Good grief," I told him, "nailed to a cross. It must have been awful."

"Awful is not a big enough word to describe my pain from the nails in my hands and feet- the embarrassment of hanging there naked for all to see and for many to shout insults-you remember I had never been circumcised. Deep gloom overwhelmed me because I would never see my mother again. Finally, I prayed for God to help me although I had never done much to help Him.

"It was finished," I thought. "My tragic life was over.

"Yells and cries came from the city walls, where a black man was helping someone carry a cross. The cross-bearer's flesh had almost been eaten away with the floggings and beating.

"'Save yourself,' I heard the bitter mobs scream at the man. They laughed and scorned him as he drew nearer.

"I was in such pain that I could hardly focus on the man who was to be crucified between me and the nasty mouthed old reprobate. Flies kept landing on my face and nose. Shaking my head to shoo away the bugs I tried to get a better look at the newcomer.

"I gasped. It was Jesus," he said.

"Why was this kind hearted miracle worker being nailed to a cross? Why did the soldiers curse him? Why did the priests spit at him? Why did the same folks who showered him with praise a few days before now mock him and insult him?

"With a giant heave, the soldiers raised the cross and with a deadly crunch the wood slid into the hole that had been prepared. Jesus groaned as the people mocked and shouted.

"With blood running down his face from a crown of thorns, he finally was able to speak.

"'Father, forgive them for they know not what they do,' he finally was able to cry out.

"'Forgive them? Call fire and brimstone down on them! Kill them, torture them, send the whole bunch straight to hell!' were my thoughts.

"But he told his Father to forgive *us*, and I realize it included me! Something moved inside me. A filthy, dirty weight began to rise from my stomach and I felt I would vomit on the soldiers below. But the strange feeling did not come out my mouth, instead I felt it change- from filth to clean, for nasty to pure, from hell-bound to a hope in heaven."

"What happened?" I asked, as if I didn't know.

Ezra stopped on our walk and turned to me. "God allows me to remember this to share with you. The physical pain was still there- two sharp nails cut through my hands like burning knifes and an iron stake had been rammed into my feet, where my blood was flowing rather freely down the wooden cross.

"I knew- I knew something wonderful had taken place- it was 'Forgiveness.' I had never forgiven a soul for anything done to me.

"Suddenly my whole body was lighter and in my mind a thing called 'Hope' began to grow. But my brain clicked in again and told me there could be no hope for me- I was a thief, a crook, a nobody, a nothing.

"The older thief screeched at Jesus, 'Hey, you stupid donkey, if you are the King of the Jews, then get yourself down off this cross- and while you are it. Get me down, too.'

"An ungodly smile came from the old reprobate that showed only a few teeth remaining in a scar scorched face. Turning his head he scowled at Jesus and at me.

“From the other side of the cross, I was infuriated that an old fool would dare speak that way to Jesus. Mustering all the strength I had left in my lungs, I cried out, ‘Leave him alone. We are getting what we deserve. But I know Him. This Jesus had done nothing wrong.’

“The old thief readied himself to hurl more cursing both at me and Jesus- when blood caught in his throat and he gagged trying to spit it out.

“Jesus turned toward me and looked with those same loving eyes I had seen when Lazarus was raised from the dead.

“’Lord, remember me when you come in your Kingdom,’ I cried; tears sweeping down my face as I realized what a stupid thing to say. If King Herod had ridden up on one of his magnificent horses, would I have begged King Herod to remember me in his kingdom? Of course not. The guards would have chopped me into little pieces for even speaking to the king.

“I wanted to apologize to Jesus for asking so much for one who had so little. But before I could construct a sentence, I heard the most beautiful words I had ever heard (and I hadn’t heard very many.)

“’Today, you will be with me in Paradise,’ Jesus said.

“I could not believe my ears. I wanted to say, ‘You have got to be kidding,’ or ‘Surely you don’t mean me, an unclean Jew, who was not even allowed to go to Synagogue?’

“But Jesus nodded his head. ‘Yes.’

“I wanted to shout ‘Hosanna’ again and wave a palm branch one last time.” but instead a brutal pain ripped my heart, I took a deep agonizing breath, looked back at Jesus, and whispered, ‘Thank you, thank you.’

"I closed my eyes and prepared to leave that old ugly cross, the filthy hole of a life I had lived in; the hatred of the crowd, the nasty world I had occupied for just a short time."

Stunned, I was speechless. I did not ask him if he floated over the cross; and I have no idea if he had to shoot through the dark tunnel and see the light.

But Ezra did tell me just before he began to vanish, "I believed and when I opened my eyes, all my filth and sins were gone- washed away NOT by the blood that flowed from my own cross but from Jesus who had been crucified with me."

And then the thief that was saved on the cross was gone, back to his place in Heaven.

Seeing an unoccupied bench beside the lake I saw down and thought. "I'm not sure how time works after death, but I do believe that when Ezra. the thief, opened his eyes, he saw the most gorgeous sight he had ever seen. Standing in the gate of the garden he saw the beauty- the mountains, the flowers, the beauty of Eden, but they dimmed in comparison to the man in white who reached out two nail scarred hands to welcome him into Paradise.

In my Father's house are many mansions:
if it were not so, I would have told you.
I go to prepare a place for you. John 14:2 NIV

MY MANSION

Robert-al appeared at my shoulder and I asked, "Uh, isn't it about time we ate something?"

"Glad you asked," he grinned. "Your family has provided a feast for you back at one of their mansions."

"One of their mansions?" I asked. "Good grief, I'm not sure I want to see what kind of habitat is prepared for me. Luckily I married Sue, and I'm sure she will receive one of the finest."

We were back at the place where it all started. Mom and Dad were there, and I could see that they had invited the rest of my family over.

I am not sure I can describe my parent's mansion. It was absolutely nothing like I imagined. My thoughts were that when we all got up here, it would be like one of those suburbs after World War II, when all the houses were exactly alike- except they would be mini-castles.

Their residence was much like the old wooden frame house we had lived in for years. The earthly one was painted white, with two bedrooms, living room, dining room, breakfast room, kitchen and one bathroom.

What I saw glowing before me was similar to that old house, except it was made of white marble, with a golden front door. Dad escorted me in and I thought I had entered the ballroom at the Biltmore House in North Carolina. It was huge, extravagantly decorated, with a chandelier that looked like the prop in "Phantom of the Opera."

"This is our living room," mother told me. "Now let me show you our dining room."

I had been in some of the castles of England, where the dining room would be so large it could be used for a basketball court- but this was unbelievable. A long, long table stood in the middle of the room, surrounded by rose colored chairs with golden trim. The plates, the silverware, the serving pieces- all were solid gold. Before me was a feast that outdid any movie version of a royal meal. There were roasts, hams, turkeys, and naturally fried chicken. I didn't dare ask if they killed the cows, hogs, turkeys and chickens up here- or if they imported them from down below.

My sister, Nelle, informed me, "Bob, honey, don't worry where all the meat came from. Nothing is killed up here. Somehow it is possible to say, 'Roast, come forth,' and there it is. It works the same ways for snacks."

"I assumed the veggies and bread appear the same way," I said.

"That's right," she smiled. "It's the same for deserts- just call our 'Lemon ice box pie, come forth,' and it appears from nowhere."

"One question," I asked my mother, "what about when the feast is over- who has to do all the dishes and take out the garbage?"

John, my brother, responded, "I figured you would ask that- because that was one of my questions. First, you need to know that there ain't no garbage in heaven- or I wouldn't be here. Secondly, you have to use that phrase your angel told you- except in reverse."

Nodding my head, I said, "Got'cha', Food, go …."

"Don't say it now," he laughed. "All the food will disappear if you say F-O-O-D, G-O F-O-R-T-H."

"We're lucky *it* can't spell, whatever *it* is," I said as I sat down in a chair between my mother and father.

I was shocked when my dad said, "Let's bow our heads for a blessing." In all my life, my quiet father had never said a blessing out loud- the rest of us had that chore.

"God, our Father, thank you the blessings you have given us. And we are grateful that Bob is now here, so we can share the good times together. We thank you for this food." "Amens" went up from all my folks around the table.

How sweet it was.

Back on earth, Sue and I had a chance to eat at some pretty fancy restaurants- because I was on a few boards of trustees. But nothing compared to this food. If anyone could duplicate this recipe for fried chicken, they would put Colonel Sanders and Chick-fil-a out of business. They told me that as I grew older my taste buds would diminish. Not in my case, nor that of any old preacher I knew. Everything on earth tasted great to me. Plus my wife, Sue, was one of the best cooks back on Earth.

You would expect the deserts to be *Angel Food Cake*, and you would be right- topped with gobs of real whipped cream, strawberries, blueberries, blackberries and a few berries I had not met before. Sprinkled with sliced almonds, it was a treat to behold. Just as my mouth was watering over the cake, more pies and puddings and ice creams arrived. I thought I had died and gone to heaven- well, I guess I had.

After the meal, which would add ten pounds to my weight down below but was sheer satisfaction up here, we gathered in the spacious living room and talked, and laughed, and talked some more.

Never in my life had I enjoyed anything as much.

Robert-el appeared at my elbow and said, "Don't you think it's time you got some sleep?"

"Sleep?" I asked. "I didn't think people in Paradise slept."

"Really? Do you think Adam and Eve stayed awake all those years they were in the Garden of Eden?"

"Well, no, but…"

"Over and over I have explained to you that Paradise is the Garden of Eden, just expanded and improved."

Looking around the mansion of my parents, I told him, "I'm sure they have plenty of rooms here…"

"Your mansion has plenty of rooms," he said.

"My mansion?" I had forgotten that Jesus said he was going to prepare one for me. There was no feeling of guilt, for it was not allowed. But I did feel something like shame, for I felt I had done so little compared to the Apostles, or Paul, or the great missionaries like Lottie Moon, Hudson Taylor, William Carey, Adoniram Judson or Jim Eliot. They all deserved the big houses along with Billy Graham, John Wesley, Martin Luther, and on and on.

My abode was just down the street and reluctantly I followed my angel. It never gets dark in heaven, so I guessed we would follow the Alaskan way of sleeping during the summer months- they went to bed by the clock and woke up the same way. It was light for twenty-four hours in that state down on earth.

We stopped before a home so magnificent I took a deep breath and said, "Good gracious. This must be my neighbor- undoubtedly he or she or they were great heroes of the faith."

Then I noticed something peculiar. The mansion looked like our house back in Argo, Alabama- just bigger and brighter.

"How do you like it?" Robert-el asked.

"Like it? I love it. Just wait till Sue gets up here, she will be as pleased as punch," I answered. "But there are so many rooms, we don't have enough furniture to fill this large a place."

"Your faith provided the home, your good works filled the rooms.

Your Faith Provided the Mansion- Your Good Works Filled the Rooms.

"Remember all the time you spent trying to help the drunks?"

"Yeah, but…"

"And remember how you and Sue tithed when you hardly had enough for food? Then how about all those missionaries you helped around the world? You were filling yo*ur heavenly home with treasure when you visited the sick, the shut-ins, the hungry, the poor, the prisoners."

"So that's the treasure we were building up. I had in mind a few chests of gold!"

"Gold is not so valuable here as on earth," he smiled. "You remember the old joke about the old man who wanted his gold in Heaven, and an angel reached down and handed him a chunk of the pavement."

"Very old joke," I smiled. "Probably dates back to the time of Ananias and Sapphira, who thought they would accumulate a lot of stock in Heaven by giving a big gift to the Lottie Moon Mission Offering."

"They gave a huge amount, but unfortunately they lied about it," he said solemnly. "They bragged to the church that they had sold their property and given it ***ALL*** in the offering plate."

"That word, ***ALL,*** is the downfall for a lot of church members. Jesus demanded ALL," Robert-el commented..

"Some would drop a dollar in the plate and expect a thousand percent increase in Heaven," I said. "Then there were those poor souls who would assure me they were saved because they believed there was a God- but never lifted a finger, nor a check book, to help His work."

"You don't have to worry about them; many of them have been removed from your memory bank. It would be too painful for you to think about those good old guys and gals who spent a small fortune to attend every Alabama or Auburn game but at the end of the year when they received the statements from the church for their gifts for the year, it was sadly low," he said. "But let's change the subject, let's talk about the good times you have already had up here. One question- was it worth it?"

"Was it worth it? You mean the few little struggles and pains I went through on earth? Of course it was. But I know now much how deserving are those Christians in China, or Russia, or Sudan, or Nigeria who were killed for their faith. I think they would quickly tell you like that old song, *It will be worth it all, when I see Jesus.*"

I walked up to the front door, looked at my name- with space for Sue's to be inserted very soon. There was a panel that stated:

I am the door:
by me if any man enter in,
he shall be saved,
John 10:9

"How appropriate," I thought as the door opened before me, like the electric doors at Walmart. I stepped into a large vestibule and noticed the grand chandelier. Then I saw something that Sue would love- on the walls were pictures of our children- when they were young, growing up, and then with their families. Beside them were our grandchildren- again with baby pix, playing sports pix, graduation and wedding pictures. It was simply gorgeous, for I told Sue many a time that we had the best looking kids in the world, until we had grandchildren, who naturally were all handsome or beautiful- as well as their spouses. The best part was that all of them were there. If one had not been a Christian- there would only be a blank.

When I entered the living room, I was astounded at the sheer beauty. It was large enough for all our family to gather at Christmas or Thanksgiving. "Hmm," I wondered out loud to my angel, "Do you, uh, we have holidays up here?"

"Every day is Thanksgiving Day in Heaven- and it is the same for Christmas and Easter. All of our days are happy, holy days," he replied. Then added, "But of course, they are not really days. This is eternity but God allows us to keep some semblance of time. It won't do you any good to count up the days or years- you would run out of fingers and toes quickly. But to answer your question- Yes. We celebrate Christmas, Valentine's Day and Easter."

"No Halloween?

"Afraid not."

"Even if we all dress up as angels?" I asked

My angel just chuckled as he said, "No."

Peeking in the other rooms, I saw beds that were king size, naturally. Each bedroom adjoined gigantic bathroom- well, that answered a question for me since I felt the need to use one of them.

As I entered one, I asked, "I am amazed we have bathroom facilities."

"They are much improved over the outhouse Adam and Eve had to use back in the Old Garden." he answered. "Plus, you will enjoy the showers and spas and baths that are available."

Moving out of the spacious bathroom, we walked toward the back of our *mansion.* There I discovered what I sought. We had looked through magazines and wished we could have afforded a larger kitchen- but what we had on earth was small but adequate. This one was a whooper. Ovens and refrigerators lined the walls, with an island full of cooking units.

"I assumed you can order your meals cooked or uncooked," I said.

"Or you can make them from scratch."

"I doubt if Sue will ever get around to seeing all the wonders of Paradise. This kitchen will be heaven for her."

"Outside is a basketball court and a swimming pool and over the rise is a magnificent golf course."

"Thanks, but you have to remember I am in my eighties with herniated discs and I can't…"

"Past tense," he teased. "You couldn't play basketball back on earth. Remember you are now thirty, a little past your prime but you still loved it. Plus, you spent quite a bit of your time after retirement playing golf."

"And the pool?"

"Standard equipment. You will enjoy it as well as your grandchildren, great grandchildren, and great, great…"

"Wait a second. Hold on, you mean I am going to meet all of my descendants? There will be hundreds, or thousands of them."

"Only if they are Christians," he said. "And only if they are born before the day comes when Jesus returns to earth. That will be the end."

"So you don't know a lot about the rapture, the tribulation, the thousand year reign, the Anti-Christ, the dragon and all of that?"

"No. We are not told the future, nor have we been given special lessons on the meaning of prophecies or the book of Revelation. We just know that then there will be a new Heaven and a New Earth."

"Whoa!" I cried. "What is going to happen to all of this?"

"Simple, Paradise will then be transformed into the New Heaven and the New Earth. You won't lose your mansion or anything in it. In fact, as I told you, you will reap benefits from the works of your children and those you won to Christ."

"If the benefits are more furniture in my mansion, I don't think we will have much room when Sue gets here.."

"It will be a different kind of reward, but I don't know what it will be. I'm just a Guardian Angel. And I doubt if Gabriel and Michael, the archangels, know much about the reward system here in Heaven. You've got to remember, you are only one of the humans that has died and come here. There are millions and millions more- and millions to come. Add to that the billions of angels we have- and you see, Heaven won't be crowded, but it sure won't be empty.

"You know, I'm not tired, but I do feel that I could use a good night's sleep- or whatever you call a night up here."

Yawning, Robert-el smiled at me and said, "We've both had a pretty busy day, as you call it. Think I'll mosey on over to my space in the angel quarters."

"Are they anything like this?" I asked.

As he disappeared, I saw his grin and heard him say, "God takes very good care of His own."

Lord, our Lord, how majestic is your name in all the earth!
You have set your glory in the heavens. Psalm 8:1

SECOND DAY IN PARADISE

I have no idea what Adam and Eve thought on that first morning they awoke in the Garden. Probably like us, they showered in a nearby waterfall- don't worry- the water was warm. Then Eve prepared a veggie breakfast, composed of berries, coconut milk- or who knows? They may have milked old Bessie. Later, they would learn to reap crops of wheat and barley, then she would prepare biscuits with eggs, (no ham for they did not eat meat until much, much later.) Some intellects state that not eating meat is the reason they lived so long- Adam reached his 950th birthday till he passed from one Garden to another. My own view is that they lived in a special Land of Eden and God protected them so they lived longer. I have other ideas on that, but let's get back to Adam and Eve on their second day in Paradise.

Most folks never give any thought to what Adam and Eve did- except of course, when Eve was tempted by the Serpent, ate of the forbidden fruit, and offered a bite to Adam.

But I don't think that happened on Day Two. My own theology is that they were there for many, many years.

So what did Adam do on day two? Simple, God had told him to take care of the land- so Adam fashioned a hoe and shovel and took off to care for the fields and the animals. I don't think he spent a fortune on dog and cat food as we do, nor did he have to buy a bale of hay for the horses. They all ate off the land- it would only be later that they would eat each other.

Eve surely took time to comb her long blonde hair and apply a little juice from the cherry to her lips, and maybe a drop of two from the blue berries to accent her perfect eyes.

But, she didn't spend all day primping- they both had work to do, so she headed out to the garden to gather food for lunch and dinner. Later she would wander through the groves of fruit trees, gathering apples, oranges, coconuts and anything else she desired. Perhaps she took a peek at the Tree of Knowledge of Good and Evil- but God had placed a "No Trespassing" sign. Since she was curious, she would look and smell- but not handle. That would happen later, much later.

Never had I slept better nor dreamed any more pleasantly. The smell of bacon and eggs made their way into my bedroom, so I pulled on a new white outfit and walked into the kitchen.

Deep inside, I had hoped it was Sue- but I was pleased that my mother had on a nice clean apron and was busy preparing my meal. Wow, how many mornings did she get up and fix my breakfast? Until I finally wandered off to college, I guess.

"Good morning, mama," I called. "I'll be there as soon as I bathe and shave."

"You don't have to worry about shaving up here," she called back. "Your father found that unless you want a beard, the hair just doesn't grow. Oh yea, and remember when I would give you fifty cents to go to town on Saturday for a haircut?"

"I remember- plus you would give me an extra quarter; ten cents for a movie, and a nickel for coke or popcorn."

"And that gave you had an extra nickel to give at church on Sunday," she smiled.

While on earth, I was a mama's boy and loved her as much as a young skinny legged boy could. But after college and marriage, I didn't send the letters as I should. Nor did I visit her very often in the nursing home- mainly because it was 250 miles away over in Georgia. But now my heart was bursting with a deep, deep love for her and my dad.

As soon as my bath was over, I walked into the kitchen in my mansion- and was still elated over how magnificent it was. Dad was seated at the table, so I gave him a hug and whispered, "I love you, dad."

On earth he had false teeth and he would often be talking to me and somehow stick out those teeth to tickle me. However, up here his teeth were not false- nor was anything else.

My plate filled with scrambled eggs with cheese, a bowl full of grits, two thick slides of bacon, a bowl of gravy and fresh hot biscuits. An assortment of jellies and jams encircled my food.

"Thanks, Mom," I said as I blew her a kiss. "Let me say the blessing this morning."

"Dear Lord, on earth I thanked you each day
for my blessings- even when times were tough.
Now I have my mom and dad back with me-
and I just can't express enough gratitude to you.
Thank you for this food.
For I pray in Jesus name,"

It was delightful to hear two Amens join mine.

+++

"What do you have on tap for today?" I asked my father.

"Same as every day, I go to work," he smiled with his real teeth.

"Work? I didn't know we had to work in Heaven, I thought we just sat around and rested all the time."

"Don't you remember what I taught you in the Bible?" mother said. God told them to care for His Garden," she asked. "Then, Adam and Eve were told to 'multiply and replenish the earth.'"

"My multiplying days are over," I laughed. "I think we did a pretty good job by adding four children and 13 grandchildren to the population."

Mother thought, then said as she pointed at my father, "Well, Robert and I did our share. We had four children, that were all strong Christians- not counting that sweet Rose Marie, your sister that died so young. Let's see now, they gave us at least twenty-seven grandchildren, and…"

"Grace, if you are going to get into great grandchildren and great-greats, you will make us sound like God's promises to Abraham," dad said to my mother.

"Uh, so what kind of work do you do every day?" I asked.

"Oh earth, I was in the lumber business, but I learned a lot about carpentry, so I help prepare the mansions up here."

"And I worked about the home and raised a garden," Mom added. "Would you like to see my tomatoes? You won't believe how large they grow."

"Well, what am I supposed to do?" I asked.

Robert-el appeared sitting beside me. It was hard to talk with a mouthful of eggs and grits, so he swallowed and said, "You were a writer so you will use those skills here."

With that, he covered a biscuit with the butter and strawberry jelly. "You know," he said, "heavenly food is great- but I never had a chance to eat home-made cooking."

"Well, you are welcome at our house any day at supper time. Usually I cook everything myself- but yesterday we wanted Bob taste Heaven-made food," mom said.

"Hey, my mother was/is a great cook- and so is my wife, Sue. So you'll have to drop by our place after she arrives. Me? I can't cook anything. I told Sue if she died before me, I would have to bring somebody home with me from the funeral!"

They all laughed. It surprised and pleased me how much laughter I heard in Heaven.

"So what's my job?" I asked my guardian angel.

"Well, we have enough preachers up here, every Worship Day."

"Worship Day?" I asked.

"Yeah, it's a little confusing. You are now in eternity but God allows us to keep our a twenty-four cycle. But it's not like the twenty-four hour schedule on each. Eight *hours* are for work; you have eight eating and being with your family. Then you have already discovered heavenly sleep. Also, God kept our seven day week, for you remember he created the world in six days and on the seventh- He rested."

"Then Christ came along, was crucified but raised on Sunday morning. From that time on, the order for most Christians was five days or work, one day to shop at Walmart, and one day to worship and be with the family."

"You get the idea. Our first day is Worship Day. That's when we gather in groups and a preacher or missionary brings us a sermon. Oh, that's after our choirs have sung- and, oh man, can they sing!"

"Kinda' like a good old Baptist church," I said.

"Plus, we have lots of testimonies. Some Christians were severely persecuted and even killed. Often some of them will share their stories and always end with, 'I forgive them in Jesus' name.'

"Everybody has a story, and sooner or later, they have the opportunity to share it with others. You will have a chance to preach, but, um, let's see, it won't be for another thousand years or so."

"I can hardly wait," I laughed. "But how will I work at writing up here?"

"I have a computer and such."

"But I'm not a well-known author."

"Doesn't matter. You wrote books about Christians and about Christ."

"They didn't sell very well."

"So what? Someday your books may become popular, and they will all become best sellers," he grinned.

"I doubt that."

"Did you know we have libraries up here?" he asked.

"No."

"Bet you didn't know all of your books are already there, and many, many people read them. When you finish this book on Heaven, it will be available at all your neighborhood libraries."

"Do I start today on this book about Heaven?"

"You have already started writing it in your head. You have a computer with all your equipment set up in your mansion."

"Where?" I asked, getting up from the table and itching to get my fingers of a keyboard again.

“That room over there,” Dad said. “I helped build it, but I don’t know anything about computers- they came along after I was long gone. I still prefer reading my newspaper.”

Opening the door to my stunning computer room, I gasped. Then I realized what my father had said, “Newspapers in Heaven? Somebody explain.”

“I thought I had told you about that. The Good News Paper comes daily and as you can tell by the name, it shares all the good news- the ministries of people and churches, the evangelism update, other good news events you might want to know from earth. You will receive your local paper- which means your news will come from *Birmingham News* and the. *Alabama Baptist*- but only the good news!

“There won’t be much good news in the *Birmingham News*, how the *Alabama Baptist* will me help me keep up with how the churches are doing.

“The most important part is what you would call the *obituary*. We call it the *Sanctuary*, and it updates you on all the people you know who have arrived here.”

“And the ones that don’t make it?” I asked.

“As I told you, that’s bad news, and it is not printed up here.”

“So, I don’t know if my worldly friend made it or not?”

“Oh, you will know if he made it; but if not, there’s no memory of him.”

“Whew, this is all mind boggling,” I said as I scratched my head. “Do I start work this morning on writing?”

“Oh no, you have time off to examine Heaven. You still haven’t been to Jerusalem.”

"Is the New Temple there?"

"Oh, no. Jesus builds that when he returns."

"Uh, is God there?" I asked.

"Yes and no."

"What does that mean?"

"God's throne is in heaven, on the great white throne. But since He is God He can be here in Paradise or Third Heaven at the same time."

"The same for the Holy Spirit?"

"Yes, but the Spirit is so busy on earth trying to kindle up revival fires, convict people of sin, convince them of righteousness, and comfort folks who has lost a loved one- like your family. The Holy Spirit right now is ministering to each and every one of them."

"That's hard for me to comprehend."

"No, it's impossible for you to understand, for much of your mind still works on earthly reasoning."

"Mom, thanks for breakfast," I said as I hugged her. "Dad, you did a first class job on my computer room, thanks. And both of you receive medals for raising us four kids- and you get extra medals for our children and grandchildren."

+++

My angel and I stood outside the walls of the Holy City. One of my fondest memories from earth was the night we came up from Jericho, passed Bethany and drove by the Mount of Olives. Jerusalem was spread out below us.

Spotlights on the walls of Jerusalem made it seem like a dream.

"Wake up, Sue," I called to her way back then. "Look there, the Holy City."

We were both so excited we wanted to jump up and take pictures with our old 35 mm camera. But the Guide said, "Take a quick look. We will be back here later on the tour. Tonight we are running late for your meal at the motel."

The Bible had given us a pretty good photograph of the Jerusalem walls here in Paradise. They shimmered and shone like a Disney World parade- there were so many jewels. Lights glittered as we approached, and I realized we really were walking on golden streets.

Unlike the cartoons with Peter sitting behind a desk accepting or rejecting people, there were angels at the three gates on each side. A huge pearl was the door, but it was pulled back so we could enter in through the round opening.

+++

Peggy, a friend back on earth, had a Near Death Experience, and she had told me what Heaven was like. Peggy was having surgery at UAB hospital, when she died, and was gone for about eight minutes. They were able to bring her back, and she told me what she had seen. Her vision was the only one I encountered where she went to her own funeral. Standing in the balcony of the First Baptist Church of Lineville, Alabama, she looked down at her casket- surrounded by her husband and two sons. They were grieving, but she felt no pain, no emotion except peace. Then she added that she was not allowed to turn her head around to see Heaven, but with the periphery of her eyes, she could see shining translucent buildings and there were people scurrying around as if going to work. She said it was beautiful. She returned to live but unfortunately, had a stroke and endured a lot of pain after her vision. She said that it didn't bother her, for she knew how great she would feel in heaven.

Peggy told this story to our Wednesday night crowd while I was at Centercrest. Now here is the extra miracle part! Judy Brewster had to work long hours at UAB hospital and seldom was able to attend on Wednesday night. But when Peggy finished her story, Judy was present and stood up and said, "Brother Bob, I know that story is true. I was the anesthetist when they operated on Peggy- and she was dead for eight minutes!"

+++

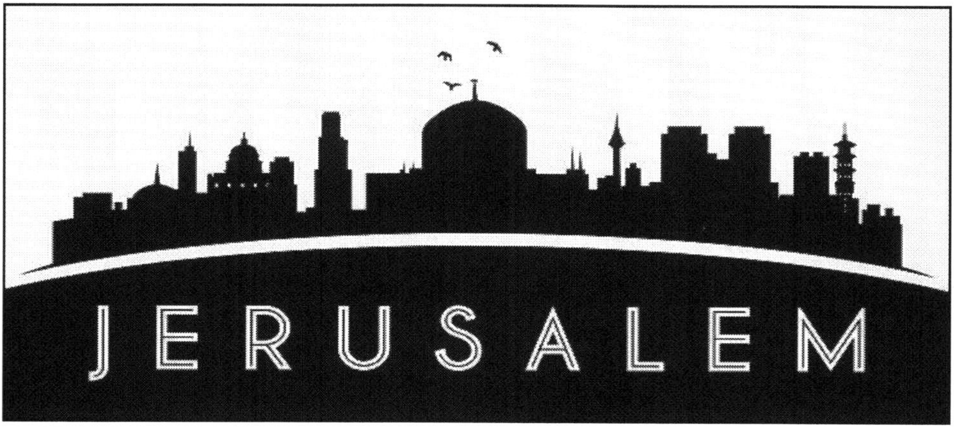

"because of the hope laid up for you in heaven.
[Colossians 1:5]

WHAT IS HEAVEN LIKE?

Maybe it's time for me to share my personal theology with you.

First, I believe people who are saved go to Paradise, or Third Heaven. The Seventh or Final Heaven will take place after the Return of Jesus and the Final Judgment.

The only descriptions we have of Paradise are:

- Luke 16:19–31: Lazarus with Abraham.

Dives (which means *rich man*) ends up in Hades, but is able to see Abraham and Lazarus (not the one who was raised from the dead, but the poor man.) Dives shouts across the great gulf and asks for Lazarus to come down with a sip of water. Abraham refuses. The tormented man then requests that Lazarus come and warn his five brothers. Request denied- reminding him Moses and the prophets had given out warning signs. Then Father Abraham states:

they will not be convinced

even if someone rises from the dead.

- 2 Corinthians 12:1-4: Third heaven is Paradise.

I know a man in Christ who fourteen years ago
was caught up to the third heaven.
And I know that this man—
whether in the body or apart from the body
I do not know, but God knows—

*was caught up to **paradise**.*
He heard inexpressible things,
things that man is not permitted to tell."
(2 Corinthians 12:2–4).

Paul told us that he was not permitted to describe the beauties of Paradise. I don't know, but the reason may be that people would be ready to pack up and head there.

Paradise is from the Greek word for *park or garden.*

There are many other references to the glory of Heaven

When I first entered Paradise, uh, wow, it was only *yesterday,* but it was *beyond description.* I tried to give you an idea what to expect, but it's like trying to describe a symphony to a deaf person or a sunset to the blind.

But as I entered the Holy City, it was *beyond description.* Yesterday the sheer beauty took my breath away- but this Jerusalem took my breath, hearing, smell and the sight out of one eye. Luckily it was only temporary.

+++

1.

PARADISE
English from the
French ***paradis,***
Latin ***paradisus,***
Greek ***parádeisos.***
Aramaic ***pardaysa***
Hebrew ***pardes***

I saw the Holy City, the new Jerusalem, coming down out of heaven from God, prepared as a bride beautifully dressed for her husband
Rev. 21:21

JERUSALEM, OH JERSUALEM- NOT THE CITY OF REVELATION

I think I had better stop and let you know that the Jerusalem of Paradise will NOT be the New Jerusalem in Seventh Heaven, which will contain the Temple and the Ark of the Covenant.

John sees Heaven in Revelation 21:10-27, but this refers to the New Jerusalem coming down out of heaven. Statistics are given: 1400 miles in length, 1400 Miles wide and 1400 miles tall- that's almost 3 million cubic miles. That sounds huge, but the earth is 260 billion cubic miles- 120,000 times larger than the new Heaven. If you are worried about defense, the walls will be 200 feet thick.

I know, you wonder if there may not be enough space for you- I have good news- those stats are only for the New Jerusalem, not the New Earth and Heavens. Those cannot be figured on a calculator for they will be endless and eternal, much like the pi, **π,** that doesn't seem to have a stopping point. Some have even suggested it represents God, for it is without end.

Just keep remembering I am in Paradise, not the Seventh Heaven.

Let me try to give you somewhat of a preview picture:

- **The Music**. Soft and sweet melodies floated across the area that were a combination of all the great Christian music on earth. Some probably was written back in the days of Christ, because the Bible tells us that they sang a hymn and went out. Was it a Psalm? A Christian hymn that Peter or someone had written? Of could it have been a musical arrangement of the Lord's Prayer?

The music was as soothing as aloe is to a bad sunburn. Sometimes it would be an angelic choir probably including a number of humans who had reached Heaven. I hate to tell you, but there were Gregorian Chants and Contemporary Music- but they didn't upset anyone. Plus there were areas where the different kinds of music were played- so you could just wander around until you found what suited you- much like people did in my last days on earth. Also, there was some way you could *pipe in* your favorite genre of tunes.

● **The Fragrances.** Often I had questioned why the three wise men showed up with one gift of gold and two presents of perfume. Also, my inquiring mind wondered why there was an Incense Altar standing before the veil in the Holy of Holies.

Undoubtedly, God likes things that smell good. He gave fragrances to flowers, fruit, and new cars. (Better hold that last one, I doubt if God make that scent- but it sure smells good to me when we could afford a new vehicle.)

Since Paradise was filled with flowers, I was aware of the aromas that filled every space I had visited. But this was not the smell of flowers- it was something more- much more. You wanted to grab a handful of it and eat it, like cotton candy.

● **The Sights.** I hate to compare New Jerusalem with Disney World, for that sounds like heresy. But the comparison would be much like the delight and joy a young child experiences when he walks through the gates in Florida and sets out to explore Adventure Land, Frontier Land, Fantasy Land and Tomorrow Land.

Sue and I had visited the Holy Land years ago and were astounded at the natural beauty. As I told someone, any which-a-way you look, it was like a Picture Postcard.

● **The Temple Mount-** Back on earth, there is no temple on Temple Mount, instead The Dome of the Rock Mosque occupies that space. Moslems flock there in droves but Jews dare not set foot on that area.

Here in Paradise Solomon's Temple shone in splendor with its white marble walls and gold trim. The sight was so dazzling that I wished I had brought my eclipse glasses with me. (By the time of Jesus, Solomon's temple would be long gone and King Herod would build a Temple there.)

The temple of Solomon stood there as my angel and I hovered at the holy site. We were allowed to walk, and look, and touch the old sites of worship. Like a first time tourist to Israel, I gawked at the columns, the courts, the Holy Place, and even saw the Veil that had concealed the Ark. We would view everything, including the great Menorah and the Altar of the Shewbread. But we could not break off a piece and eat it! The Altar of Incense was as close as we could get to the Veil and the Ark. I wanted to view the Ark of the Covenant and its contents, but Robert-el held out a hand to stop me. You will have to wait until we were the Final Heaven to view the Ark.

Outside I stood amazed at the thirty foot long altar where so many heifers, lambs, doves and pigeons were sacrificed. The blood had been shed so freely. But now there was no squawking of birds, nor mooing of cattle, nor did the lambs *bah* there a last good-bah. Jesus' sacrifice had put a stop to all that. Now there were only stones placed carefully together and a million dreams of what it must have been like back then.

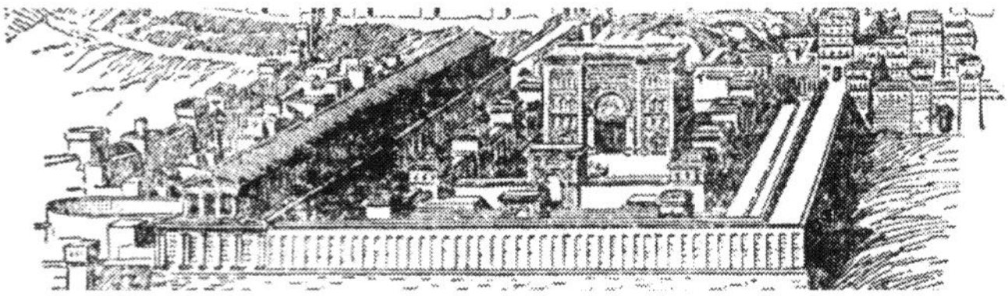

He is not here; he has risen, just as he said.
Come and see the place where he lay.
Matthew 28:6

CALVARY AND THE EMPTY TOMB.

Slowly the scene changed from the time of King Solomon to the time of Jesus. It was a real surprise when we walked up to Golgotha and found only one cross still standing. There was not even a hole in the ground where the older thief had taunted Jesus and begged to get him down. Amazingly the final abode of the young thief also left no pieces of wood, no nails, no blood. Instead there grew a rose bush, filled with flowers, indicating that he was not there, he was in Paradise.

The Center Cross still stood. It was empty and there were no blood stains streaking down the sides. Nor was there any inscription written above indicating that this was the King of the Jews. The reason was obvious, Jesus was King of the Universe- they gave him too small a title.

Walking up to the cross I reached out my hand and touched it. An electric shock went through me- oh, it didn't hurt, it was more like when the Holy Spirit would fill me at a revival or when people would be saved.

Standing there, I wanted to burst into singing, *The Old Rugged Cross,* but whoever was in charge of music beat me to it and the most wonderful arrangement of the old hymn came drifting on the breeze. Robert-el stood there, knowing the powerful emotions swelling up inside me. It was here, at the cross, where I first saw the light and the burdens of my heart rolled away.

I had preached about the cross and about the One who was crucified there. But to stand here and behold the spot where the blood was shed and my sins were forgiven almost moved me to tears.

My angel reminded, "Hey, remember- no tears in heaven."

"If I could cry, they would not be from pain or grief, they would be from the overwhelming event that good place at the cross. He didn't just die for me, but for everyone. How I wish more people would have accepted his pardon and accepted Him as their savior. They could stand here with me at the cross in Paradise, instead of being blanks in my memory."

He put his hand on my shoulder, and it was like my mother calming me down at night when I had a bad dream, or was sick, or just not feeling good. There came forth a feeling of victory and peace.

"May I see the tomb?" I asked.

"Sure," my angel said, "but you know He is not there."

I smiled, "Thank God, He is not there. Had he not risen from the grave, he could never have gone to prepare a place in Paradise for that young thief or for this old preacher- and millions and millions more."

It was a short walk down the side of Golgotha to the tomb. It was hard to tell if this was the Garden Tomb that Sue and I had visited- or as the Catholics and Orthodox think in the center of the Church of the Holy Sepulcher. When we were there on earth, not only was the tomb empty, it was gone. Pilgrims had broken off chunks of it over the thousands of years. Nothing is there now except a shrine when they say Jesus was buried.

I often told my church members that it doesn't really matter WHERE he was laid to rest, but WHAT he did that mattered. He rose from the dead, conquering death for all of us believers, and rolling away the stones that kept us out of Paradise and Heaven.

The tomb looked a lot like the Garden tomb, with its small opening where we both had to bend over to enter. There was the shelf on which His body had been laid.

On earth, as I stood at this spot, I was moved, but the guide had watered down anticipation as he told us the Garden Tomb may be the resting place for Jesus, but probably not. I had been inspired by that experience long ago, especially as we existed the tiny room, we saw the sign, *He Is Not Here, He Is Risen.*

Back then it had been a cloudy day and we had sat in a small amphitheater overlooking the door to the grave. As we were sharing the Lord's Supper, a shaft of light broke through the clouds and spilled across the open door to the empty tomb. Now that was goose bump time.

My angel and I examined the empty ledge, then I asked, "Why are we the only ones here? I would have expected thousands crowding in here all the time."

Robert-el smiled and said, "Oh, they are here. You simply cannot see them- nor can they see you- or the others. We felt that the cross and the tomb need to be kept to just one or a few beings able to see it at one time. However, since time is different here, you need to know that right now there are countless people from all nations gathered here to experience the power of the cross and glory of the empty tomb."

"May I come back and show Sue when she arrives?" I asked, hoping that I didn't have just a one-time ticket.

"Sure, and you can bring your children, and grandchildren- and I can assure you that you will experience the awe you felt now each time you return. You won't get bored with the cross nor the tomb."

● THE MOUNT OF OLIVES

"Hey, before we leave here, there another place I want to visit, " I told my guardian angel. Although I didn't feel I needed a Guard, I still needed a Guardian.

"Sure, it's right over there, we can see it from here," he said.

"I keep forgetting you can read my mind or maybe you just made a lucky guess," I teased. "From where we are standing, we can look back to the East and see the Mount of Olives."

"A lot of folks want to visit there," he said.

"You told me that I can't see them, how many are over there right now?"

"Several thousand, but they won't bother you, we'll just buzz over and take a look."

Instantly we stood in the grove Sue and I had visited years ago. But something was different. When we were there, the trees were old- in fact. there was one that was reported to be over two thousand years. Our guide told us Jesus may have knelt there to pray and I had suggested maybe that was the tree where all the disciples fell asleep like they still do in church. The tour group had laughed but our Jewish guide didn't catch the humor.

"This is the tree that celebrated its two thousandth birthday when you walked here on earth," Robert-el said.

The trees were green, with that neon glow that all living plants have here in Paradise. And hanging like tiny Christmas ornaments were plump green olives.

"Are they ripe?" I asked, wanting to pick one and take a bite.

"No, these would turn reddish, then purplish and finally black."

"I guess I'll just wait then, because I love black olives- the green ones are too sour."

Walking past the tree, I saw a huge flat rock. “Is this where Jesus prayed?”

“Yes.”

“But all our pictures showed him praying as he leaned against a huge boulder.”

“I wasn’t here that night, but I did see a full picture of the evening. Jesus didn’t bow down on one knee to pray, he fell down on this rock and sobbed and prayed.”

Looking at the exposed piece of granite, I wondered what the terrible night must have been like. “Say, can I call up someone to this spot?”

“Sure, go ahead.”

“Simon Peter, come forth,” I cried out.

And there he was, just about like I had pictured him. Bronzed from his fishing days, he stood tall and muscular. His dark curly hair was down to his neck and a short tangled beard adorned his handsome face.

This time I learned to be quick, so I jutted out my hand and said, “Simon Peter, I’m glad to meet you. Believe me, I’ve heard a lot about you.”

His big smile broadened as he gave me a bear hug and had we been back on earth I feel several vertebra would have popped. He held me out at arm’s length and I realized how tall he was. In my basketball days, I was listed at 6 foot, three inches- although I think I have shrunk.

“Brother Bob,” he said in a somewhat husky voice, “I have looked forward to meeting you and chatting.”

“Really?” I asked, feeling it hard to believe someone like Saint Peter would want to talk with me.

“Yes, it’s about that play you wrote about me years ago.”

"You know about that?" I asked for I had almost forgotten it myself.

"Sure, it was entitled, *The Rock,* and I loved your intro-diction- *"Jesus Christ and Simon Peter and the disciple I can't name, born about the same time, but when the three rocks collided, it changed history and the setting of time."*

"Wow! I am impressed! Had I known you would be in the audience I would have tried to do a better job," I said meekly.

Changing the subject like the wind altering its direction, he asked loudly out, "So you want to know what happened here that night?"

"Well, yes," I said sitting down in a bench.

Peter plopped down beside me, as my guardian angel waited sitting on the branch of an olive tree.

"It started back in the Upper Room, you remember," he recited. "All us disciples were bubbling over with enthusiasm. The next day, Friday, would be the big day in Jerusalem with over a million Jews gathered there. I still believed he would proclaim his Messiahship, set up His Kingdom and boot the Romans out on their royal *fannies.* Just in case He needed any help, I had my sword strapped at my side. I carried it all the time, and I'm sure Jesus knew, but He never rebuked me for it.

"Mary Magdalene and Mary, the mother of Mark, prepared the Passover lamb- and it was delicious. We were almost giddy thinking about tomorrow- and, as Jesus promised in his prayer to us, *Thy Kingdom come, thy will be done, on earth as in heaven.*

"James and John were horsing around and singing a silly little song about one soldier defeating a whole army with just one sword."

Scratching his head, Peter said, "Somehow I think there was somebody else at the table. I know there were twelve of us, but I can remember only eleven. *Somebody* was as sour as a cucumber and actually holding his hands to his ears to keep out the sound. I didn't know then, but Jesus knew, that *somebody* had already sold out his Master for thirty stinking pieces of silver. Hey, you could buy your own prostitute for that amount. Finally Jesus whispered something to whomever that was; he scowled again and went out.

"Whoever it was betrayed Jesus, but there are many theories as to why. Some that *somebody* sold him for the money, others say that it was to force Jesus to become King. The Bible makes it clear- the devil entered him.

"Jesus took a piece of bread, a big oval portion, and stood up. We knew he was dead serious, when he gave thanks and broke it, and gave it to us, saying, '*This is my body given for you; do this in remembrance of me.*'

"We had no idea what that meant, but he started tearing off pieces of bread and giving them to us. He paused at each disciple, looked deep into their eyes and whispered, '*I love you.*'

"Then he picked up the Elijah cup, the extra cup we have at Passover believing Elijah will return just before the Messiah. We blinked as he said, '*This cup is the new covenant in my blood, which is poured out for you.*'

'We drank it, paused then a fight broke out between the two sons of Thunder, James and John, as to who would be greatest in the new Kingdom.

"I started to jump in, whip both of them and declare myself as the General of all God's Army, when Jesus set up his kingdom. I forgot that Michael, the archangel is head of God's militia.

"Good gracious, this sure sheds new light on the first Lord's Supper," I said as I shook my head.

"Yeah, I still wonder sometimes why Jesus chose us. Five of us, James, John, Philip, my brother, Andrew, and me- all came from a little known fishing town called Bethsaida. There were only about two hundred people living there. It was nothing special and we sure didn't think we were in an extraordinary group. I had no idea why he chose me."

Robert-el saw that this conversation was going to take a little while, so he reached out, created a chair and sat down in it. He said, "You need to know that everyone up here wonders why God chose them. It's like none of God's children deserve Him as their Father."

"It's called humility down on earth- and not everybody has as much of it as you angels," I said.

Peter stood up, stretched his mighty arms, twisted his neck and I could swear it heard it pop. Then he sat back down and said, "I'm not going to go through the whole night with you, for I know you remember his prompting us to fear not, and them promising us a mansion that he was going to prepare for us.

"Naturally, we all thought he would build our great houses in Jerusalem, which would become the capitol of the world."

"I know the part where he told you he was the way, the truth and the life, and no one comes to the father except through him," I said.

"You might not remember that he preached us a pretty long sermon that is recorded in the Gospel of John. Then he led us up here to this very spot."

He stood and walked over to the exposed rock. "They called this area Gethsemane in our day, it meant an olive press where they squeeze every drop of oil from the olive. That's what happened here, Jesus squeezed every drop of emotion from his body," he said as his smile faded. It wasn't sadness, it was more appreciation.

"He left eight of the disciples as an outpost- but he motioned for James, John and me to come with him. I think he meant for us to pray for him and with him.

"He went a little further into the grove- we saw him fall down on this rock and begin to pray. So we prayed and prayed- for about five minutes. Then we three fell asleep. Some watchmen!

"He came back once, woke us all up, and chastised us," the fisherman disciple said. "Ow, that hurt. He didn't fuss at us very much. Of course we promised we would stay awake and pray, and we did, for about ten minutes that time.

"We woke when, oh, that somebody whose name I can't remember, led a group of temple guards up into the garden. Yuk, he even went over and kissed Jesus. Now that was something none of us had ever done- and that somebody didn't kiss our Lord for appreciation or honor- but to identify Him as the one to arrest.

"I was so angry I pulled out my sword and took a swipe at one of the soldiers- aiming for his neck, but he ducked and all I did was slice off his ear. I didn't know that his name was Malchus and he was the high priest's servant. Frankly, I didn't care, I just wanted to protect my Lord."

I said, "I remember that Jesus told you to quit- he touched the ear and healed him. I suppose his hearing went back to 20/20- or however they count good hearing. On earth I didn't hear too well and my wife was always after me to get a hearing aid. I informed her that I was not going to spend four thousand dollars on hearing aids, which I would use for five minutes, tire of them and put them in a drawer somewhere. My reason was that I had rather give the money to missions."

"Amen," Peter said. "It amazes me how people of earth spend their money on things they don't even need while there are those who have never heard about Jesus."

"Good heavens, what a terrible night," I said as it dawned on me all that happened. "How can you remember those things when all our bad thoughts are removed?"

"Gethsemane was a place of suffering, but God worked it out for good," Peter said.

"How was that?" I asked.

"Jesus praying," Peter said as he disappeared back into his part of Paradise. "**Not my will, but thine**."

Looking to my angel, I asked, "Is my interview over?"

"Peter doesn't like to talk about all that happened the rest of the night- his denial of Jesus, his running away, his absence at the Crucifixion,' Robert-el said.

"Hmm, I can understand that," I said as we went traveling back to my house, my mansion. Somehow I was hoping Sue would be there to welcome me.

My huge home was even more beautiful, and I imagine if Loneliness was allowed in Paradise, I would have had a good case of it.

+++

| Thou hast been in Eden- the garden of God;
Ezekiel 28:13

THE GARDENS

"Would you like to see the Gardens today?" Robert-el asked as he floated over the bottom of my bed the next *morning*..

"See the Gardens? I thought we were in the Garden," I sleepily replied, rising up on one arm.

"Well, you are in the Garden of Eden expanded into the Garden of Paradise- or Third Heaven, whatever. But you really need to visit the gardens Adam and Eve built while they were in the earthly version."

"Never heard of them," I said as I climbed out from under the solid white sheet and equally white bed spread. I slept in my white outfit- but it never seemed to get soiled. Maybe there's no dirt in Heaven, but I put on a new one each day- which always seemed to be freshly laundered with a scent of magnolia and honeysuckle- pressed to perfection.

"Sit down and eat," my angel suggested, "and I'll fill you in on your great, great grandparents in the Garden."

Breakfast was waiting- but this time it seemed heaven made instead of mama-made. There was a hot cup of coffee with cream and sugar standing guard over a Belgian Waffle, filled with strawberries, whipped cream and something that looked like little lumps of dough.

"O.K.," I said. "Thanks for the meal and I recognize everything but the little white M and M's."

"Guess!"

"Let's see, we have blackberries and blueberries up here. Is there such a think a white berries?"

That set him off giggling again. "You really freak me out with your questions?"

"Freak out? What kind of terminology is that for an angel? Are you supposed to go around saying, 'Fear Not?'"

"Oops, maybe I slipped," he said sheepishly. "We have to keep up with your languages down on earth- and your idioms. Imagine what we think when we hear you utter such phrases as:

1. *A penny for your thoughts*
2. *See eye to eye*
3. *Kill two birds with one stone*
4. *To hear something straight from the horse's mouth*
5. *Costs an arm and a leg*
6. *Speak of the devil!"*

"Now that you mention it, I had trouble with Spanish idioms- and Hebrew and Latin and Greek idioms. Come to think of it, I had trouble with the whole language."

"Right, and to give you a hint, those little white blobs on your waffles are **manna**, *the food of angels*."

Biting down on a few, I said, "These are really good. Why did the Hebrews complain?"

"Same reason you would complain if you had to eat a Belgian waffle every morning for forty years."

"It figures," I said and finished my meal, and licked the platter clean.

And the LORD God planted a garden eastward in Eden;
and there he put the man whom he had formed.
Genesis 2:8

A TOUR OF THE ORIGINAL GARDENS

The original Garden of Eden was a special place- it was a colony of Heaven on earth. Adam was put to work- and he tended the animals and the crops- but he also spent a great deal of time constructing some special gardens- and we have left them just as they were," Robert-el told me as we arrived at a section seemingly of Paradise I had not visited.

THE GARDEN OF PEACE

We wound around the narrow trail as greenery surrounded us, and felt as if we were wandering through a tunnel into the deepest jungle. Ahead we could hear wind chimes- soft notes composing a melody. Suddenly we emerged into a quiet meadow. Sunlight painted the clouds with every pastel shade, yet left the sky behind a soft mellow blue.

Flowers bloomed all along the edges of the lawn- as well as hanging from the trees. Every shade of gold mingled perfectly with pale blues and violets and soothing greens. In the center of the garden a calm lake stretched out lazily across the landscape. Several willows dipped their lacy branches toward the cool, clear water. Two swans slowly made their way across the placid scene like two ballerinas tip-toeing across a stage.

All was still. All was quiet- except for the gentle sound of the wind chimes.

"Whew! I've never experienced any place like this on earth. It's too bad Adam couldn't leave this behind for all of us to enjoy. It's so, uh, beautiful. So peaceful. I feel I could stretch out here and sleep for a year."

"What is this place? Does it have a name?" I asked

"The Prayer Garden of Peace," my angel whispered.

"Well, it sure beats going into a closet to pray," I said. "I feel a great urgency to talk to God."

Robert-el smiled like a teacher when his students finally discover some great truth. "When we come into the presence of God there is a natural desire to pray."

I said, "Hey, there's something by the willow tree. I'll go look and see what it is."

A low bench sat silently beside the willow. I examined it, shook it, then set it down again. "If it's a sitting bench, it must be for midgets. It's not high enough."

"Don't you remember when you visited the Catholic church?"

"Yea."

"And you couldn't figure out why they would stand up, sit down, then kneel down on those funny little benches."

"Oh, this is the Prayer Garden- so this is a prayer bench. I suppose Adam must have made it. I doubt if Eve could nail two boards together."

He said, "If you'll look, there are no nails, only pegs."

"I doubt if she could peg two pegs together, either."

Examining the work surface again, I nodded my approval as if I were a judge of fine furniture. Then I knelt down upon it and found myself not *praying*, but actually *talking to God.*

After a time of *praise* and *thank-you's*, I looked up and Robert-el was smiling. "Why isn't prayer that way down on earth," I asked, remembering how whenever I tried to pray my thoughts ran off in a hundred different directions, and then I had to grab hold and pull my mind back to the subject of my prayer. "This was more like a chat-room, or a real person to person meeting."

"That's the way it was supposed to be," he answered,

"So this is the Garden or Prayer and Peace. How about this for a pithy saying, 'Prayer is the Pathway to Peace.'"

Standing, I saw something under another willow tree. "What's that? Another prayer bench?"

My angel smiled, "It looks more like an-answer-to-prayer bench for the sheep and goats. It's a feeding trough."

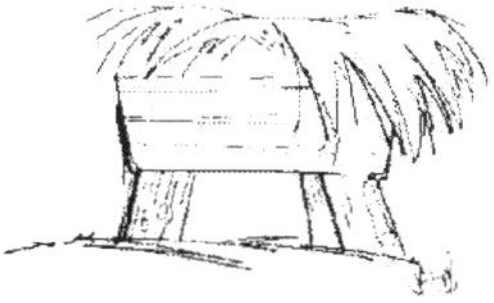

I walked over, pushed the drooping limbs of the willow back and knelt down beside the newly found object. "A feeding trough? Adam probably brought his flock here to feed them and allow them to rest in green pastures beside still waters."

"Oh, I remember," I said as the music seemed to change to a Christmas medley. "A feeding trough is a manger. But what is this doing in the Prayer Garden of Peace?"

"Maybe Adam prayed for his sheep?" the angel grinned.

"There's more than that, and your know it," I said. "The Prince of Peace was born in a manger."

My guardian nodded agreement. "But do you remember what the Angels sang that night?"

"Peace of earth," I said. "Peace on earth, good will to men! I think I get it now, this manger/feeding trough is a sign that mankind would fall, fail to eat from God's feeding trough and lose this tranquility - but in the future the young Prince of Glory will come back to bring peace back to planet earth. That is just beautiful. Oh, I love this place. I can see why people who have after-life experiences and visit Paradise don't want to come back home."

The chimes begin to play again and my angel jumped to his feet and began to dance. He swirled through the branches, then swayed beside the tranquil pond. Feeling the music, the two swans glided gracefully toward him swinging their heads to the beat of the music. When he finally finished his impromptu ballet, I applauded.

If you could blush in heaven, Robert-el surely would turned a bright pink. Instead he explained, "I can't sing well enough to be in any of the angel choirs, but I did learn to dance."

"Hey, you could probably make a million dollars on the television show, *So You Think You Can Dance."*

"I don't believe they would approve of my music."

"Oh, I don't know, Heather Whitestone danced her way to Miss America with the tune, *Via Dolorosa,*" I said. Then I added, "Did you know I had her at my church three times- and once two of my granddaughters went up and danced with her?"

"Of course, I know that," he said. "Who do you think prompted her to ask for two volunteers and who whispered in your ear to send up your two darlings?"

"Ah, I thought that was my own doing," I confessed.

"Well, it was your own decision, because you could have refused my suggestion."

I pondered over that for a while and then answered. "Some of these days, I want to sit down with you and let you fill me in on all of the times you whispered in my ear or made some suggestion that turned out right."

Grinning, he turned away from me and said, "Well, most of the time. But let's go explore this path that leads from the Garden of Peace to another one of Adam's creations."

■ THE PRAISE GARDEN OF JOY

Without waiting for an answer, I raced across the grass and down a path leading through the woods. It felt so good to be rid of back problems and lung damage and other old age illnesses. It only took a few minutes to reach the opening and walk through.

Robert-el grabbed my arm as I gazed in wonder at the scene before me. I had been to Yosemite and gawked at the waterfalls and mountains. But they were nothing compared to what stood before us. Mountains of lavender and purple stood like Royal Guards in the background. Waterfalls in every shade of green and blue floated to the ground. Mists rose from them and hovered out across the Garden, watering every plant.

I shook my head in disbelief of the beauty. Then I told my angel, "There were no rainbows in the mists in Adam's day. God didn't create them until the time of Noah. If you look closely, you can see shades of blue and yellow and red- God's DNA in His Creation."

Pools glittered beneath each cascade, and the water gushed out and over rocks, splashing a merry tune as it flowed along. The previous garden was one of pastel colors- this was one of bright shades. Fire red rhododendrons banked the edges of the creeks, brilliant orange azaleas grew wildly, lemon day lilies surrounded tropical flowers. The scene was so happy, I beat my chest and let out a Tarzan call. Robert-el laughed and thumped his chest in an effort to mimic Jane.

"What is this place called?" I asked.

"This is The Praise Garden of Joy. Adam and Eve would come here to laugh and run and romp like children."

"So Eve came here?" I asked.

"Sure, but she never learned to enjoy it like Adam," Robert-el said sadly. 'Eve was always wondering what was on the other side of the mountain. Sometimes she would tell Adam she wished there were more geraniums in this garden- or often she would bring exotic plants and place them beside the gurgling waters. The next week she would dig them up and plant them somewhere else. In the last days she wanted to climb the mountains and ride down the waterfalls to experience a greater thrill. When Adam told her it would be dangerous, she would reply that they were in God's image and nothing could hurt them."

"Well, that was Eve's problem!" I said. "I am going to enjoy this moment." I leaped into the rushing waters. The creek seemed to be aware of my presence and burst forth with a happy tune. Robert-el and I looked across the gorgeous garden and began to sing an old song with a rather peppy tune:

Joy to the world! The Lord is come:
let earth receive her King!
Let every heart prepare him room
and heaven and nature sing.

Joy to the earth! the Saviour reigns:
let men their songs employ
while fields and floods rocks hills and plains
repeat the sounding joy.

Slowly, I swayed with the music and added a threefold "Amen" at the end.

Robert-el watched from the bank. It did him good to see God's child so happy. His eyes misted over as he remembered the good times Adam and Eve had sung a similar song, danced the same dance and felt the same elation.

"This is what God wanted and still wants for his creatures," he said. "God existed in the Trinity for ever- before angels and before the big bang. He did this with Love, Joy and Peace. That's what helped him through eternity. Imagine if you were with your son and your Spirit, and all of you shared Love, Joy, and Peace with each other- all the time. That would be Heaven. He created the angels to share those feelings.

"Much later, he built a Garden in the East of Eden. He filled it with trees, animals, flowers and a man and a woman. But he meant to fill them with enough Love, Joy and Peace that they could be happy forever. But that dream was shattered into a billion pieces when they disobeyed and ate the forbidden fruit.

For ten or fifteen minutes- earth time- I laughed and rollicked in the garden and the creeks. To me it seemed an eternity of bliss. Finally I wandered up the creek toward the falls and found a surprise behind a cave. I called out for my guardian to come and see what I had discovered. He waltzed through the falling water as if it were the first snow fall of the season.

I pointed to the wall of the cave and said, "I didn't expect this. It's wider than I would have thought. And what is it doing in Eden, especially in the Garden of Praise and Joy? Can you explain this tomb, my dear angel?"

He walked over to the empty tomb and sat on the ledge cut smoothly into the cool wall. He motioned for me to sit beside him. Putting his arms around me, for the first time he felt like my big brother, instead of just an angel.

"Gabriel explained this to me on my first trip here," Robert-el said. I was stunned for I never thought the idea of death would cross your grandparent's minds- well, not until the day they ate and fell. Adam heard God very clearly when He told them the day they ate of the fruit of the Tree of Knowledge of Good and Evil, they would die.

"Adam was smart- he knew Eve and he knew it was not 'if' but 'when.' So he slipped up here and made a tomb for two.

When Eve ate the fruit- she would die. It would bring pain and sorrow into the Garden just as Lucifer did in Heaven. Adam would bring her body here and lay her down in this grave. Then he would eat the fruit and lie down beside her.

"Eden, without Eve, would not be Paradise."

"So that's the reason he ate the fruit with Eve," I said.

He answered, "That was part of the reason, but Satan tricked both of them. They both ate- they both sinned- they both died."

I thought a moment and said, "Wait a minute, they both didn't die..."

"Yes, they did," he answered. "They looked as alive as angels in heaven, but when they disobeyed, they lost their eternal lives- and you remember they also lost their garden, their home."

"But why is this tomb in the Praise Garden of Joy?" I asked.

He thought a moment then said, "Bob, ask that question again- but include the word, 'empty.'"

I blinked at him, puzzled, then asked, "Why is this *empty* tomb in the Garden of Praise and Joy... Oh, I get it. I see. Our joy today comes from the fact of the empty tomb. Easter. Resurrection. He is not here, He is risen. I love it."

Jumping on the ledge I made an imaginary microphone with my fist and said, "Ladies and gentlemen, I bring you good tiding of great joy. For the savior who was born in a manger and who died on the cross is no longer dead. The death tomb is empty- He is alive forever more!"

With that Robert-el let out a war hoop that echoed back and forth in the cave. "So folks, we can have real joy because Jesus rose from the grave."

■ THE GARDEN OF LOVE

First, we encountered the Prayer Garden of Peace." Robert-el told me as we walked toward another path that led through the trees toward a third garden. "Secondly, you experienced the Praise Garden of Joy."

Pushing aside the orchids and ferns that blocked my way, I took a step inside and said, "This has to be the Garden of Love." I inhaled strong fragrances pulsating toward me like rays from the sun on a summer afternoon at Panama City Beach.

Before us stretched gardens of roses; brilliant reds, calm pinks, assortments of yellows and golds and dazzling whites. Alongside them was every mixture of rose you could imagine, along with some colors I know I have never seen on earth. The fragrance of a million roses filled me with an ecstasy I had never known.

A path stretched before us and continued up and over a small hills.

"I felt a lot of love when I first arrived in Heaven," I said as I reached over and gave my angel a big hug. "I love you, man, uh, I mean, Robert-el, uh,,,

"How about brother?" he said to me. "You didn't know I existed but I was always there, protecting, providing.

"I'm the twin brother you always wanted. I have always loved you- and always will."

Feeling a bit embarrassed- for hugging on my counterpart so long- I finally dropped by hand into his and said, "Thank you."

"Oh, you've been fun to work with- you were always doing such crazy things to win people to Christ.. Your plays, your books, your special services, on and on," he grinned. "When we angels would get together, inevitably one would ask, 'What strange thing has your pastor done now?

"I told them of the night you had the Lord's Supper out in the garden at the church- and how the grape juice has been bought a month early and left to ferment. When those old Southern Baptists took a shot of the *welch-grape-juice-turned-to-wine*, their eyes lit up.

"Then you had one of your deacons, hanging on the cross- they removed him and he was to make an up-from-the-grave appearance- by appearing on top of the building that stood behind the cross. All went pretty well, except you used fire extinguishers. With a whoosh, you had some guys spray them up into the air- the man playing Jesus stood magnificently between them1"

I started laughing, choking out, "It wasn't funny at the time, but I didn't know that the extinguisher material is heavier than air. So there stood my actor, with two fire extinguishers going full force, but instead of rising into the air, the substance ran down the side of the building and almost choked us."

Both of us were laughing so hard, I had to sit down on the pathway.

Then it hit me- a short pain to the heart. Grabbing my chest I looked at Robert-el and asked if we have 911 up here.

His smile vanished into one of deep concern, "No, we don't need Paramedics. But I know what caused your hurt."

"But how?" I asked. "You told me all our pains, and sins, and hurts were left outside the Garden Gates."

"True, but sometimes a little root, a tiny reminder remains. In certain circumstances it can erupt in a sharp sting. Do you remember any of it now?"

"Vaguely, while they were in the acts of crucifying Jesus that night, a deacon whom I thought was my friend, screamed out, 'That ought to be Bob Curlee being nailed to the cross.'"

My archangel walked over and put his protective arm around me. "Yeah, I know," he said softly. "It hurt me and a lot of people who didn't know how to respond to such demonic talk."

Looking up at him, I smiled, "Although we never mentioned the act, I forgave him- but, it took a long time. Now I can't even remember what or who it was! Thank God for Heavenly Memory Loss."

We walked up a small hill and I was surprised at what I saw.

It was a cross!

Looking at Robert-el, I asked, "Why did Adam build a cross here in the Garden of Love?"

"It seems of all people, you should know the answer to that one," he said. "The cross stands for the greatest love mankind has ever experienced. The very Son of God gave his life for us, and he did this because He loved us."

"How could Adam know this?"

"He didn't. Your great, great grandfather was working on this the day before the fall. It was really the first part of a gazebo he wanted to build for Eve. But all he finished were two boards pegged together."

"So," I said as I walked up to touch Adam's last attempt at carpentry, "if we are to see the cross in all of its beauty is to picture it as our salvation from a tsunami or sin and evil. Yet to see it now," as I reached out and touched it. "surrounded by the very best that flowers can offer- it stands above, apart and alone in its majestic beauty.

We stood there for a while, soaking in God's glory, then I spotted the carving near the foot of the cross. Written in some language I didn't recognize, it reshaped itself and spelled:

I ♡ U

"Ah, how sweet that was of Adam to write that to Eve

"Adam didn't write it."

"Eve wrote it""

"No, who was the only One who could have come back into the Garden after the gates were closed and guarded?"

"Jesus wrote that to… us?" I asked.

"That is His signature on the cross," Robert-el smiled as if he had just shared with me the purpose of life.

"Wow, all these years, theologians and scientists have been attempting to discover how the world was made. They didn't take time to take a close look at the special world God made- the Garden."

Turning away from my angel, I said softly, "Uh, there's something I need to know. Uh, is there love, uh, sex in heaven?"

"Let me tell you a story," he said as he plopped down on a bench. "A little boy asked his daddy, 'Is Sex better than Chocolate?'

"The father looked wild-eyed at his wife and finally said, 'Well, son, sex and chocolate are two different experiences."

"Pretty good answer," I said.

"That's my answer to you- sex on earth and sex in heaven are two different experiences!"

"Enough said," I grinned. "I guess I'll just find out some day."

+++

I saw heaven standing open and there before me was a white horse,
whose rider is called Faithful and True.
With justice he judges and wages war. Rev. 19:11

THE CHARGER

We left the gardens and were sitting outside under a tree, enjoying the coolness of the day when all of a sudden there was a loud "Whoosh."

"What was that?" I yelled as something flew past me so fast-all I could see was a white blur disappearing in the distance.

"Not to worry," Robert-el said as he finished off a barbecued rid.

"Not to worry! That thing could have killed me."

"No, it can't- you are in heaven."

"Surely it would have broken bones, dislocated limbs, fractured my ribs," I said.

"No, no, no, no," he answered as he reached for my chest. "No damage, just a big fright.

I stood up and looked where the white blur had disappeared.

"Better watch out!" my angel warned. "Here comes another."

Sure enough as I turned, I saw a flash headed toward me. Jumping nimbly on top of the table, making sure I didn't step in the French fries, it went by like a low, very low, flying jet plane.

"O.K., Mr. Know-it-all, what were those two things that just sped by?"

"Oh, we call them Chargers," he said, licking off his fingers.

"Chargers! The only kind I know is the ones I have to plug into my cell phone or I pad."

Looking at me, he grinned, "Those chargers of yours are to put energy back into your phone, etc. These are different."

"Tell me about it! How could you catch one to plug something into it?"

That was funny to him. "Don't you remember the stories from the time of King Arthur when Knights would mount their *Chargers* to go capture a fair maiden from the dragon?"

"Well, yeah, but, what are war horses doing in Heaven?"

"Come on, don't you know there is a terrible war between Good and Evil; between the forces of God and the allies of the Devil?"

"Ha!" I said, "there is no way Satan can sneak back into Paradise- is there?"

"No, but he is going wild down on Planet Earth. You had best pray for your family and friends. The dark clouds of war are forming and the winds of terror are being felt- even in your country."

"Come on, you sound like an announcer on CNN," I said. "Sure, our politics and entertainment seem to be going crazy- but at the heart beat of America can be found any Sunday morning in thousands of churches in the good old U.S.A., and around the world."

"I hate to tell you but it looks like the world is headed toward Hell-in-a-Hand-basket- and remember you have loved ones down there who are Christians, but who are not immune to Satanic attacks- neither is America."

"I thought we were not supposed to talk about bad things up here, only good," I said.

"True, but we can mention evil if it results in good," Robert-el looked around, then whispered to me, "I have special permission to show you the work of Satan on earth- but only because you are writing a book about this. But you have to promise you won't tell anybody."

"I promise, I promise," I answered a little fearfully. "But I'm so accustomed to life in Paradise, I don't know how I can handle the culture shock of earth's evils."

My angel led me a few miles or a thousand miles, who knows? Finally, we stopped before a huge wall that stretched up into the clouds (yes, they have clouds and gorgeous sunrises in Heaven. But there are no sunsets.)

There was a building beside a humongous gate. Inside I could swear (except you can't swear in Heaven) that I heard the sounds of hundreds or thousands of horses, or as my angel calls them, Chargers. Robert-el knocked on the door and a massive angel stepped out. I recognized him immediately, not because I had seen him before, but because everybody knows each other up here.

"Gabriel!" I smiled and held out my hand.

He returned my smiled and shrank down to a little over six feet tall, took my hand, and said, "I'm glad to meet you, Brother Bob."

"Brother Bob! Wow, that is a supreme compliment coming from you. By the way, I would like to ask you a few questions about the Virgin Mary. Was she frightened when you appeared to her and announced she would be the mother of Jesus?"

Robert-el punched me in the side and said, "We don't have time to talk. Gabriel is the Arch Angel Messenger of God, and he has the authority to show you the message from down on earth."

"O.K., O.K.," I said, "it just that you don't get to meet someone like Gabriel every day."

Motioning to enter his building, I looked around at the unbelievable technology around me. All I can compare it with would be the old James Bond movies, where the villain sits in a circular room surrounded by television sets of maps and events all over the world.

"Just a moment," the Arch Angel said, and flipped off the lights. Immediately we were surrounded by scenes that would make all nine of the Texas Chainsaw Murders look like play dough.

Before me, a group of terrorists were laughing and jeering at a group of young girls cornered in a church. As I watched, they pulled out machetes and began to whack the screaming young ladies into pieces. The next set showed jail cells in China where pastors were being kept and tortured for theirs faith. Babies were coughing and bleeding in a hospital in Africa- the result of chemical warfare. Then America zoomed into focus- and I was shocked to see Nazis fighting Blacks in the streets of Birmingham, my old home town. Tanks came into view and cannons exploded ripping into buildings and people. Scenes of serial killers and child abusers filled some of the screens.

Turning to Gabriel, I said, "This is what can happen in the future, right?"

"No, this is happening right now on earth. But here is the worst part." North Korea filled a huge area, and then telescoped down to where missiles stood- and men were busy loading nuclear bombs onto them."

"Nooo!" I cried. "Gabriel, speak to God, and let Him stop this insanity."

Suddenly a scene of a small church appeared. Smiling families sat together and sang,

I'm satisfied with just a cottage below
A little silver and a little gold
But in that city, where the ransomed will shine
I want a gold one, that's silver lined

I've got a mansion just over the hilltop
In that bright land where we'll never grow old
And someday yonder, we'll never more wander
But walk on streets that are purest gold

Hundreds of screens came to life with people worshipping God in huge cathedrals, in unpainted churches, in brick buildings with a cross held high. As I marveled at the faith of people back on earth I saw scenes of people hiding in basements- jungle people singing what sounded like *The Old Rugged Cross*. On and on and on pictures of the faithful were shown to me- from packed arenas to a few worshipping in a small country church.

"Magnify by millions what you see and you have a picture of the church, the body of Christ on earth," my angel said. "That is what is holding back God's wrath- dedicated Christians like you and your wife and family. There are millions of them down there. They are the shield that is holding back the End," Gabriel told me.

"Well, that's O.K. for a hundred years from now. But how are those saints making it through their times of persecution. Good grief- a nuclear war would be horrendous. Our government would be gone, electricity, water, banks, schools. How in this world will my family deal with all of that?"

The scenes changed to hundreds of church all over the world- red and yellow, black and white- and they were singing the same tune, but I recognized the this well-known, often-song hymn.

Amazing Grace, how sweet the sound
That saved a wretch like me,
I once was lost, but now I'm found,
Was blind, but now I see.

As I watched, Gabriel grew larger and larger, until his head was in the clouds. I shouted up to him, "When? When will God end all this misery?"

A thunderous voice called back to me, "I don't know- not even Jesus knows."

"Quick, Robert-el, get me out of this place. It's been so long since I have been exposed to such demonic acts, I can't handle them very well."

"Sure," my angel replied and led me out the door.

Peace fell over me like a warm summer rain. It felt so good, I wanted to jerk off my heavenly clothing and go skinny dipping in a nearby river.

"Don't even think about it," he said.

Scratching my head, which now had more hair than I had the last fifty years of my life, I asked, "What happened in that building? It's all blank. Must have been pretty bad, because all I can remember is asking Gabriel about Mary, and we entered the door. Then nothing."

"Remember I told you that bad memories and news are blocked out of our minds up here."

"But didn't you tell me that you would show me something so I could write it down?" I asked.

"You are correct, but God will block all of that until it's over."

"Until what is over?"

"Until Lucifer's party on earth is over, the last fat lady, the woman on the dragon, will sing her last song."

"Will it be 'Amazing Grace'," I grinned.

"No, it will be probably be something like 'Gloomy Sunday,' the song that led so many to suicide:

Sunday is gloomy, my hours are slumberless
Dearest the shadows, I live with are numberless
Little white flowers will never awaken you
Not where the black coach of sorrow has taken you
By Rezső Seress and published in 1933.

Shaking my head at the sadness of such a song, I smiled and said, "Maybe most of the world sings a song where they changed the lyrics a bit."

Hell! Hell! the gang's all here,
What the Hell do we care?
What the Hell do we care?

Robert-el gasped, "They actually sing that down there?"

"Oh yeah," I said, "and there are a million jokes about Hell, including one I liked- where a demon welcomes a newcomer to Hades and asks, 'Smoking or non-smoking?'"

"No! Surely people don't joke about Hell," he said.

"All the time. In fact, many will tell you that they had rather be in Hell with their drinking buddies down there instead of with a bunch of old fuddy-duddies up here."

"Unbelievable!" he said. "They must not know the horrors of eternal punishment."

"The truth is, they don't believe in Hell anymore," I answered. "And their idea that to go to heaven, all you have to do is die."

He sat down on a low flying cloud, put his head in his hands and asked, “How did the world go so wrong?”

“Sin,” I answered as any preacher would. “It started the day Adam and Eve disobeyed God, and has stretched down through the years to where men not only do not obey God, they shake their fist in his face and deny him or curse him.”

We turned to go back home, and as I breathed in the sweet fragrances of love, joy and peace, I heard rumblings behind the great wall- and wondered what they could be.

+++

For to me, to live is Christ and to die is gain. Philippians 1:21

SUE'S LAST MINUTES ON EARTH SEPT 30, 2017- 1:00 pm

Sue Curlee was driving north on 1-59, just south of Trussville, Alabama, when the first pain hit. She jerked the car to the left, but then pulled back onto the four lane highway. After about 100 yards a gigantic throbbing hit her heart and it was over. Her left hand hung in the steering wheel causing the little red P.T. Cruiser to lurch to the left, spin around in the highway, plunge down the embankment and smack into a tree.

She looked down at the wreck and was concerned that someone had been hurt- but she felt no sorrow, no pain. Looking closer she realized it was her little car. "What am I doing up here." she asked out loud.

"You are up here with us," a voice answered. "I'm Sue-el, your guardian angel. We are here to escort you to Heaven."

"I came along this time," a kind masculine voice said and she turned to see Jesus holding her hand. He winked and said, "You were a special lady to me on earth, now I want to escort you home."

"What about, my children, my grandchildren?" she asked. She felt no grief- only peace.

"I promise I'll take care of them," he said. "And I'm going to let you see a preview of your coronation."

"My coronation?" Sue asked.

"Don't you remember when you were in England, and Bob introduced as the queen mother?"

Sue laughed, "He was so funny- and so loving. But- why a coronation for a nobody like me?"

"Oh, but you were so very special. Look at that crowd! Over 1000 people came to your coronation/funeral. And to be honest, it was one of the most beautiful I have ever seen."

Sue said, "That my son, Robby. What a great job speaking. That's his daughter singing- what a beautiful voice. That guy with the beard and ukulele- that Jamey's son, J.B. What a choice for his voice, 'Somewhere Over the Rainbow.' He did a special concert for me just a few weeks ago.

"Wait, that's my youngest son, Jamey, and, my goodness he is preaching a sermon!"

"He's preaching about you and what an encouraging message you were to help everybody," Jesus said.

"Wouldn't you know it? He's giving an invitation- just like his daddy would," she said softly.

"Are you ready to go," He smiled at her.

"As Bob always would say, 'I'm prepared to go- but not quite ready."

Sue could feel the powerful love she had her family as she turned to the darkness. "Will there be a light at the end of the tunnel."

"I am the light," Jesus assured her. "We have better hurry, you've got a lot of family waiting for you."

"Will I miss my family below?" she asked.

"It won't be so much missing them as much as anticipating them joining you."

"Well, O.K.," she said as she noticed the purple bruises on her arms had disappeared. She was young again. "Bob will be waiting on you," Jesus smiled. "You had 58 wonderful years together below- get ready for eternity with the one you loved."

And God shall wipe away all tears from their eyes;
and there shall be no more death, neither sorrow, nor crying,
neither shall there be any more pain: Revelation 21:4

MY QUEEN OF HEAVEN

"Wake up, sleepy head," Robert-el yelled at me as I was just beginning a wonderful dream about my family gathered at Christmas- and how much I loved all twenty-three of them, (that's counting Sue, me, our four children, our in-laws, our thirteen grandchildren and three grandsons-in-law.)

Rubbing the sleep out of my eyes, I remembered in my latter years that I had no trouble sleeping, I just had trouble waking up and getting up. But I slipped into my heavenly suit, pulled on my socks and shoes- saluted my Guardian angel, and said, "Ready and at your command, sir."

"Hurry, we don't want to be late," he said as he pulled on my sleeve.

"What about breakfast?"

"I brought you a bag of manna," he said as we literally flew out the window. Normally we walk around in heaven, it just seems so natural. We can fly if we need to get somewhere in a hurry- and undoubtedly we move at the speed of light.

Popping pieces of the heavenly bread in my mouth as we flew along, I called out, "This is really good, but I guess I can see how the Israelites got tired of it after fourteen thousand, six hundred days in the desert."

"What?"

"That's forty years counted as days on earth."

"Oh, you are right. You would probably be slipping off at night to makes deals with Ahab the Arab for some eggs and toast, and maybe a cup of coffee."

"You are probably right," I called back. "But where are we going and why the haste?"

"You will find out soon enough," he said and we were standing on green, green grass.

+++

"Hey, I recognize this place. It's right inside the Gates to the Garden. This is where my family had gathered to meet me when I arrived. It must be somebody kin to me! Oh, Lord, don't let me have the bad thought that something has happened to my children or my grandchildren."

There were the sounds of trumpets and I could swear an orchestra was playing the Hallelujah Chorus.

Slowly there appeared before me an angel and our Lord Jesus. They were all smiles, holding out their hands as if someone were between them.

"Am I supposed to guess who's there?" I asked my angel.

"Just be patient."

Then she appeared- it was like rainbows gone wild and sunrises dancing jigs. The music increased and I held my breath in awe.

It was my wonderful wife, Sue. Finally she was here, and I took off like the old commercials where a man and woman are in a field and they rush toward each other and embrace.

"Oh my sweetheart," I said. "You have just made my Heaven complete!"

Her million dollar smile beamed back at me, "I have missed you, a lot."

Uncertain as to whether we were supposed to kiss in heaven, I threw all caution to the wind, swept her up in my arms, and kissed her like never before.

"Wow!" she said. "It's good, good, good to be home."

A group of people had gathered behind me- her welcoming committee. Holding her hand, we walked over to where her sweet mama and daddy were standing. I hardly recognized them, because they were all thirty years old now- and her mother looked a lot like Sue. They embraced and hugged and laughed and carried on like they hadn't seen each other in thirty years- which was about right.

Sue then turned to her daddy, hugged him around the neck and told him how much she loved him.

James Lenox, her father, never talked a lot on earth, and when I married into the family, he was a sweet, kind Christian man. He would say, "Hello," "How are you?" and that was about it. Sue had told me of his background where he actually sold moonshine, was not a Christian, did not attend church, and could be pretty strict and rough with his eight children.

So I was surprised when he hugged Sue again and again; then looked at me and asked, "Did she ever tell you about that Monday?"

Looking at Sue, she shrugged her shoulders, so I asked, "What Monday was that, Mr. Lenox?"

He smiled that sweet deacon smile of his and told this story: *Sue's Miracle Monday.*

+++

"Behold, now is the accepted time; behold, now is the day of salvation"
(2 Cor. 6:2)

SUE'S MIRACLE MONDAY AS TOLD BY SUE'S FATHER

I don't remember the date, but I do remember it was a Monday in 1951- not a good year for sharecroppers like me. To add to my misery I had hepatitis, was confined to a bed, where I felt like, uh, well, Hades. Plus, back in those days I had a terrible temper and would lash out at my five sons and three daughters if they did anything to bother me."

He continued, "It started on the Sunday before *That Miracle Monday*. Sue was 16 and happy as a lark. She came back from church singing- she was the only one of our family that was a church goer. All afternoon, she read her Bible and sang, "Jesus Loves the Little Children," until I thought my head would split wide open. To make matters worse, Vacation Bible School started on Monday morning and she had been asked to teach the Junior girls. If that wasn't enough for the little concrete block church, they scheduled a revival every night of the week.

"We lived in a three room house which many would describe as a shack. That's not much space for a family our size, eight children, and we had to be careful not to stumble over each other. As I said, I was feeling ill and grumpy- Sue kept singing and humming, until finally I blurted out, 'That's enough! No more singing. What's more, young lady, you are not going to teach Bible School tomorrow, you are going to stay home and help your mother!'

“Well, she started crying, went to the bedroom and slammed the door. My wife rolled her eyes at me as if to say, ‘You shouldn’t have done that!’

“But she knew better than to talk back to me because I could curse her and use a belt as easy as the eight children we had.

“I didn’t sleep good that night; the pain grew worse; my headache was throbbing; and I might have felt a little guilt about lashing out at Sue- but I was stubborn- I would not apologize and I would not go back on my word.

“Morning came with nothing any better- and no prospects for me a pore country farmer. Looking out the window, I saw Sue slip around the house with an old paper sack. I knew what she was doing- she was going to defy me- go to Bible School- and if I wouldn’t let her come back home, she had put some underwear and a flour sack dress in that bag, and she would just take her few belongings and try to find a place to live.”

+++

"At just the right time, I heard you. On the day of salvation, I helped you."
2 Corinthians 6:2 (NLT)

SUE'S MIRACLE MONDAY AS TOLD BY SUE CURLEE

Sue picked up the slack as she gave her father a hug and continued the story.

"After breakfast that Monday, I didn't speak to my daddy, because I knew he would forbid me to go teach my class of girls at V.B.S. Instead, I grabbed my Bible, hugged mama, and dashed out the door. It was a two mile walk up the dirt road to our little church, but that morning I think I ran all the way.

"After all the pledges and songs, I took my girls out under a tree. There were sixteen of them, many of whom had never set foot inside a church. We sat on the grass and I began by telling how I had asked Jesus in my heart when I was only four or five. And He came in. But I waited until I was nine, and the water was warm in the creek, before I was baptized. They all giggled.

"Then I began to teach them the Bible study for the day. They were so attentive; hungry like kittens who had been taken from their mother. All of a sudden, one of the little nine year old girls stood up, came up to me crying, and said, 'Miss Sue, I want Jesus to come into my life.'

"Stunned, I really didn't know what to do- but what happened next really got to me. All the other fifteen girls came up weeping and asking me to help them ask Jesus into their hearts. So I said a simple prayer and they repeated it after me.

Lord, I ask you to forgive my sins.

And I want Jesus to come into my heart

Then they all ended it with a sixteen voice, "Amen."

"I had never been so close to Heaven in my life- and could hardly wait for that night at the revival, when all sixteen of the girls would come forward to make their professions of faith.

Dancing all the way home, I almost forgetting about my father's demand that I not go to Bible School that day. The sack was still in the bushes, and when I entered the house, it was quiet. He was not asleep- but he just looked at me- not scolding, not demanding I leave. So I breathed a few breaths of air and went back into my room.

"After a while, there was a knock on my door, and I hesitated to open it, expecting the wrath of my daddy. But it was my sweet mama. I will never forget what she said, 'Susie, there is so much talk about what is happening at the church, I want to go to the revival tonight.'

"At first, I thought that was wonderful, because I didn't know if she had ever been to church, except for maybe a funeral or a wedding.

"I told her that was wonderful, then she floored me, 'Your daddy is sick, and if I go to church, you will have to stay home with him for me.'

"Crushed! I thought I had to be at the revival to see those girls join the church. Surely Mama didn't know what she was asking. But instead of blurting out, 'No, I will not stay with my daddy and you can't go to church,' I heard myself saying, 'Sure, Mama, I'll be glad to stay here so you can go to the revival.'

"So Mama dressed up in the best she had, which wasn't much because we had almost nothing. Thanking me, she went out the door to catch a ride on a wagon to church.

"At first, I thought I had made a great sacrifice, but as I sat in my room, I got angrier and angrier at my daddy. Finally, I threw the door open, walked up to the side of his bed, and said,

'Daddy, you have five sons and if they all go to Hell, it will be your fault.'

"Of course, I started boo-hooing and ran back to the safety of my room. There I cried and bawled- then I heard someone else crying. Carefully, I opened the door and peeked out to see what was happening.

"Daddy was crying, and when he saw me, he said, 'Sue, will you tell me what I need to do to get saved?'

"Isn't God wonderful?

"Of course, I led him through the brief prayer and he said as loudly as his weak voice would say, 'Amen.'

"Stepping back, I said, 'Daddy, you know you will have to be baptized?

"'I can hardly wait,' he said through his tears.

"But That Monday was not over yet!

"Later that night, we heard the mule clogging down the road, then heard it stop while mama got off and started to the house. I could hardly wait to tell her about Daddy's being saved- but when she came through the front door, she called out to me, 'Susie and James, I got saved at the Revival tonight.'

"When daddy told of his conversion, my mama sat down on the bed beside him and they laughed and cried like a couple of teenagers.

"Before the week of Bible School and Revival was over, almost all of my family had made professions of faith. The others came later. One of my brothers became a preacher, two became deacons, and my younger brother became very active in church in his older years

"Daddy became a deacon in the church and was one of the foundation stones. He was sitting in his chair, studying his Sunday School lesson for the next day with his Bible open on his lap. He had a heart attack, slumped over and never made a sound. (* We have evidence that Sue had the same type heart attack- it hit and she died.)

"Roberta!" Sue cried out and rushed to meet her old sister who died a few years ago. They hugged like a dear old couple that hadn't seen each other in fifty years. "Oh, I've got so much to talk about- and so many wonderful memories to explore.

"It would have been a full circle except, we don't know about Albert," she told me.

"Albert," I cried out. "Wait a minute! *If* you can remember his name, then he was saved."

+++

THAT IF THOU SHALT CONFESS

WITH THY MOUTH THE LORD JESUS,

AND SHALT BELIEVE IN THINE HEART

THAT GOD HATH RAISED HIM

FROM THE DEAD,

THOU SHALT BE SAVED.

ROMANS 10:9

For the wages of sin is death;
but the gift of God [is] eternal life through Jesus Christ our Lord.
Romans 6:23 -

SUE'S MIRACLE MONDAY AS TOLD BY BOB CURLEE

From the shadows emerged a good looking young man- with a smile like president toothpaste and a big dimple in his chin to match the handsome ones in his cheeks.

"Albert," I cried out! "You made it, you made it!"

Grinning, he led a lady over to me, shook my hand, and said, "Yep, I made it by the skin of my teeth, or I guess you can say by the blood of Jesus."

All of us were pleased- but shocked. Albert lived on the wild side and became a card carrying alcoholic. So did his wife, Nell. We invited them to church and they would always be kind and say, "Some of these days, some of these days."

"What happened?" I asked.

"Don't you remember?" he grinned. "I was in the Veterans Hospital in Birmingham, Alabama, and you came to visit me. Tuberculosis had set in and I think I was still in quarantine, but you marched right on into my room, shook my hand, and spoke kindly to me.

"We chatted for a few minutes, then you asked me about my faith. I told you I had been baptized when I was young, but that didn't satisfy you. You asked if you could share the plan of salvation with me?

"I agreed, and you pulled out a Four Spiritual Laws booklet and led me through it. Then I saw that I was a sinner and since the wages of sin is death, I needed someone to forgive me. You told me about Jesus and how he offers us his gift of salvation.

"Then you did a strange thing- you reached in your billfold, and held out a dollar bill to me. You said, 'Albert, this is a gift to you but it's not really yours until you do what?'

"I didn't know the answer and I said, 'Earn it?'

"You shook your head, 'No,' and I didn't know what to say. You kept urging me to come up with the right answer, until I finally said, 'I don't know, you will have to tell me.'

"You held the dollar bill to me as I lay in that hospital bed and you said, 'Accept it.'

"Puzzled, I agreed and took the bill into my hand. Then you said, 'That's it, Albert, you have to accept God's gift of salvation- and this is done when we accept Jesus as our Lord and Saviour.'

"I looked at the bill and realized what you were saying. Then you took my diseased hand in yours and led me in asking God to forgive my sins and for me to accept Jesus as my Lord.

"You asked me if I meant it, and I nodded that I did. You congratulated me just as the nurse came in, found you there and told you that you would have to leave.

"Since I live up in Morgan County, way out on a country road, you never saw me again before I died. So you didn't know if I was sincere, or just trying to get rid of you," he laughed.

"Sue and I were at your funeral," I said. The preacher said some good things, but you are right, I didn't know if you had made a 'death bed confession' or if it was the real thing."

Albert grinned and said, "It was real, and the best part if that Nell later accepted Christ and joined me up here."

Nell stepped forward and I said, "Nell, we visited you in the apartment where you lived a few months before you died. You shared with us your love and devotion to Jesus."

A great shout went up and as I turned around. It seemed as if half of Heaven had turned out to hear the wonderful testimony of my wife, Sue, and the miracles of salvation in her family.

+++

"Susie, I want you to meet your brother, Matthew. He only lived for three years- and that was before you were born," Pa Lenox said.

Shyly, almost like Boo Radley from *To Kill a Mockingbird*, a man stepped forward, He held a hat in his hand and smiled at both of us.

Sue grabbed him and hugged him like he was one of her own babies. "You look handsome," she said. "just like my daddy and your brother, Jimmy."

"And you look just like mama," he said as his blue eyes twinkled.

"You two are welcome to come over to our house for supper," Ma Lenox said.

Seeing Sue's approval, I said, "We'll come, but only if you have that skinny fried chicken you cook so well and some of those biscuits that are the best in the world."

Blushing, Ma Lenox said, "Well, you always told me my cooking was heavenly, so I guess you'll have a chance to find out."

With hugs and kisses the family finally tore themselves apart and there were just two of us standing there.

"Hey, this is just like we started- me and you against the world," I said referring to an old joke we shared.

"Not quite," Sue said, as she snuggled up beside me. "We have my family and yours- and piles of old friends who got here before we did."

"I know you want to go see some of your old Judson College buddies, but first I want to take you to see our modest little mansion."

As we started down the road, a large group of men and women met us. A lady who looked like she might have been from Africa said, "Sue, you don't know us, but your gifts to missions through the years, helped missionaries tell us about Jesus. We know that when you were in college you had almost nothing, but you gave your tithe and a special gift to Lottie Moon. So we thank you for your gifts and your many, many prayers."

Suddenly there stretched out before us hundreds or thousands of people and waving and shouting, "Thank you, Miss Sue, for your prayers; thank you, Miss Sue, for your gifts."

She turned to me and said, "I would cry, but there are no tears in heaven, what should I do?"

"Rejoice!" I said. "You and I wanted to go as missionaries, but they would not appoint us because of my asthma, even though you had finished college and two years of medical school. You took it in stride, gave birth to our four children, then went back and got your Masters so you could teach and help be a missionary to children in public schools."

She waved back and blew kisses to the crowds and they cheered her on.

Soon they began to disappear and we decided to head on home. "I know you will be disappointed, for your expected a mansion over the hilltop- but you know just to have a cottage up here is enough."

"I don't care about houses," she said. "It is enough just to be with you and my family and Jesus."

"I'll drink to that," I said. "Not close your eyes as I take you up to see our little humble shack."

"Now," I said and she looked and gasped.

"Bob, it is beautiful. We don't deserve such a mansion for we did so little."

"Undoubtedly, God or some angel keeps score- and this is what we have. Wait till I show you the inside, you will absolutely be shocked out of your socks."

Looking down, she said, "I don't have socks, only sandals."

"How cares?" I asked.

Grabbing her up in my arms, I carried her over the threshold and into our heavenly home.

It just don't get no better than that!

+++

Lord, our Lord, how majestic is your name in all the earth!
You have set your glory in the heavens.
Psalm 8:1

OUR HEAVENLY HONEYMOON

After the Lenox family dinner where everybody ate and talked at the same time, we finally decided the "sleep" time had come and we went back to our house.

Sitting next to each other of a solid white couch, I asked, "Do you want to take a look at the Rogue's Gallery of Grandchildren?"

"All of MY grandchildren are in the Book of Life," she said.

"I know," I smiled as I hugged her. "If it hadn't been for you half of our children would probably be in Prison."

"Jesus is the reason they are in the Book of Life," she said.

+++

Sue-el, Sue's guardian angel, met us the next morning and said, "Would you like breakfast in bed?"

"No, I don't think so," I answered, "there would be too many crumbs on the sheets."

"We don't have crumbs in heaven," she said. "In case you haven't noticed there are no mosquitoes, gnats, flies, fleas, ants, and no snakes. Also there's no garbage, no litter, no empty coke cans littering the roadway. No graffiti, no marches, no demonstrations, no gripes and no complaints."

"I can live with that," I said as I helped my beautiful wife out of bed and into the luxurious gown she was to wear that day. "You know that you are more beautiful in heaven than you were on earth."

Giggling, she said, "Is that a compliment for Heaven or a complaint on how I looked on earth?"

"No, no. Don't you remember how when you were eighty years old, people would stop you at Walmart and tell you how gorgeous you were?"

"Sure I remember, but I never did believe them."

We had eggs Hollandaise, blue berry bagels, juicy sausages and cups of coffee- Sue, black- mine with two sweet and lows and a little cream.

+++

"What would you like to do today?" I asked, realizing that "today" is not a real word in Heaven any more than 'night time" or "day time." But God let us keep a concept of time because without it, we would be lost as a ball in high weeds.

"I met Jesus when I came through the gates, but it was simply a welcome, a hug, and then he disappeared," she said. "So I think I would like to meet Him again and have a chance to talk for at least a few minutes."

Sue-el said, "Wow, you know He is the busiest person in Heaven, because everybody wants to talk with him, thank him and praise him. But we will give it a try. Has Bob told you how to summon someone?"

My wife looked at me and I shrugged, "Hey, we've hardly had time- you just arrived *yesterday*. Then we had supper, went to bed ..."

"You can stop right there," she said. Turning to her guardian angel, she said, "I would like to see Jesus."

Sue-el grinned and said, "Sure, but let your husband tell you how to call someone up."

Standing there, I just grinned, finally she said, "O.K., please, please with brown sugar on it, tell me how to call someone up."

"Glad you asked," I said. "Do you remember how Jesus called Lazarus back from the dead."

"Sure, he said, 'Lazarus, come forth."

Immediately Lazarus stood before us. Smiling, he reached out his hand and said, "Miss Sue, I am so thrilled to meet you. We have heard about the great missionary work you performed through your gifts and prayers."

Shaking her head, she said, "You really are Lazarus. But how in the world, or how in heaven, do you know about me?"

"Oh, we keep up with all the prayer warriors. You had hours and weeks and years or prayer accumulated. But, uh, your husband didn't pray as much as you did."

"Guilty," I said, "but I did help lead a lot of people to Christ."

Instantly another great crowd appeared. Lazarus said, "You are right, you were weak on prayer, but you were bold in your witnessing, in your sermons, in your plays and in your books."

"We love you, Brother Bob," the crowd began to chant.

"Also, you and Sue both gave sacrificially through the years to missions. One Christmas, you only had a hundred dollars and you gave that to a mission offering."

Waving back at the crowd, I saw so many that I had baptized and I wanted to stop right there, go over, and hug every one of them.

Lazarus read my mind and said, "Good to meet you, Miss Sue and Brother Bob. But you really wanted to meet someone else."

Poof! They were all gone and just the two of us stood there.

"So," she said, "if I am to meet Jesus, I have to use the same form, but put in His name?"

"Right!"

Closing her eyes dreamlike, she said softly, "Jesus Christ, Son of the Living God, come forth."

Opening her eyes she saw him standing there. There was no mistaking the face, the beard, the mustache, the hair, the eyes. There was a glow around him that I had not noticed with others. Instantly, Sue fell to her knees as if to wash his feet. Instead, she kept saying, "Thank you, my Lord; thank you, my Lord."

Naturally, I fell beside her and repeated our words of gratitude.

We felt his hand on each of us, urging us to rise. Then he said, "I should thank you for the work you and your family did for me on earth."

Somehow I didn't see that coming. Maybe I had expected a royal, "You're welcome." But for our Lord to thank us for what little we did on earth was unthinkable.

Let me take a minute to further describe the scene. Jesus was tall, muscular, and handsome. I could see how many of the women were drawn to him, but I could also tell that his real attractiveness lay inside. He wore a glittering white gown with gold bands on the sleeves and around the bottom of his robe. Folded over his shoulder and around his waist was a material of gold and crimson. On his head was a crown, solid gold, that said, "King of Kings." Diamonds and other jewels decorated the head piece.

His physical presence was overwhelmed with his spiritual being. As I said, a glow radiated out from him, that smelled of love, joy, peace, patience, kindness, gentleness, faithfulness and self-control.

Never had I felt to loved. Sue had the same reaction. Finally, she said, "Jesus, is there anything I can do for you?"

The million dollar smile emerged and he said, "You already have done everything you could for me."

Then placing a hand on our heads, he said, "Bob and Sue, I tell you once, but I want repeat, 'Well done, good and faithful servants.'"

Then he was gone to welcome another million people to Paradise.

We both stood there amazed and exhausted. Finally, I said, "Do you remember that old song, 'It will be worth it all, when I see Jesus?'"

"Funny, you should mention that, because the song went whirling around in my head when he touched us."

"Anybody else you want to see?" I asked.

"Not for today. Anybody else would be quite anti-climactic."

"Then, let me show you Heaven. There are millions of places to go and millions of people to meet. I don't think I will get bored up here."

"Don't I remember you saying that you were afraid that heaven would be boring for you, but that I would love standing around all day praying and reading the Bible and listening to preachers?"

"Guilty as charged," I said. "But, thank goodness, I was wrong. Heaven in the most exciting place in the world- oops, the most exciting place *anywhere and everywhere*.

+++

Over the next few days we talked with Mary, the mother of Jesus. Then we had a great time with Mary Magdalene, when I told her that in *The Da Vinci Code*, the author had her marry Jesus and the two of you headed off to France to have a family.

She laughed a contagious laugh, shook her head and said, "Jesus was my Lord, not my boyfriend. Why didn't that author suggest that Mother Nature ran off with Father God and started a family in Africa? I can assure you, it was an honor to follow Jesus- remember he cast demons out of me. There was a big, ugly one named *Lust*. He was the first to go and I never invited him back in."

Then she told us of the excitement of arriving at the tomb that first Easter morning.

"Dewdrops sparkled like diamonds and spring flowers clapped their leafy hands as we neared the place where they had laid my Lord. He was gone. We didn't know what had happened to him. Finally I heard someone approach me and I assumed it was the gardener.

"Jesus said to me, 'Woman, why are you weeping? Whom are you looking for?'

"Dazed, I didn't recognize my Lord and said, 'If you have taken him away, tell me I will take him away.'"

"When he called my name, I recognized him- he had been resurrected from the dead."

Smiling, she disappeared.

Sue and I had the time of our lives. We visited the pyramids back in time and actually saw them laying the stones for one of the seven wonders of the ancient world. Then we headed out for the ancient city of Nineveh- then the modern state of Alaska-

Sue loved that place when we visited. It was snowing and we sang Christmas carols.

Every day with Sue was sweeter than the day before

+++

Building the Pyramids

But we are citizens of heaven, where the Lord Jesus Christ lives.
And we are eagerly waiting for him to return as our Savior.
Philippians 3:20

IT'S TIME

"Get up, get up, Sleepy Head, it's time," my guardian angel, a.k.a. an alarm clock, yelled at me.

I looked for my watch and remembered we didn't have them up here, but I figured I had only been asleep three of four hours. Scrambling out of bed, I stretched my arms and legs, wiped my eyes and looked at him. He was literally doing a dance in the air, he was so excited.

"What's happening?" I asked praying that North Korea had NOT dropped an atomic bomb and at the same time offering up prayers that the USA had not bombed them, or Russia, or anybody.

"It's time," he shouted again and reached beneath my bed and pulled out a box I didn't know was there. Opening it, several objects glowed.

"A sword?" I asked. "Surely you don't have swords of Weapons of Mass Destruction up here."

About the time I had the words out of my mouth he pulled out what looked like a medieval suit of armor.

"Is this some kind of game we are going to play, like the Baptists versus the Methodists in a simulated sword fight? And the winners take on the Catholics?"

"No, this is the real thing," he said. "Hurry, let me help you get everything on. Over my chest, he pulled a gold plated breast plate, then tied a golden belt around my waist. I was beginning to see a pattern, when he put on my golden shoes and handed me a shiny shield that looked as if it were made of pure diamonds.

As he placed a gold and silver helmet on my head, I caught on. "This is the armor that a Christian needs to wear."

"*Needs* to wear?" he asked. "A Christian *has* to wear this armor or the devil will conquer him and leave him as roadkill."

"So? Is this a quiz? We would do this often at my church, I would yell, '*Armor Check!*' And everyone would rise and repeat with me as they acted it out, 'Breast place of Righteousness,' 'Belt of Truth,' 'Shoes Swift to Carry the Gospel.' Then we would hold our out arms and shout, 'The Shield of Faith.' We would place on our heads an imaginary hat and call out, "The Helmet of Salvation."

My angel smiled, "I loved it, every time you performed that ritual. But hurry!"

"Wait, you forgot the most important piece," I said as I held out my gleaming sword. "Then we would all hold up our hands and recite, 'Take the sword of the Spirit, which is the word of God.'"

"Sure, I know."

"Is this like a fire drill or a dress rehearsal?" I asked.

"No, this is the real thing!" he said as all of his armor appeared on him, complete with his sword.

Then I heard the rumble that quickly escalated into the sound of a hundred tornadoes rushing at us. Opening the windows I looked out and saw Him.

Jesus was riding a magnificent white horse- quite different from the lowly animal his mother rode into Bethlehem to give Him birth. This was a whole different league from the donkey on which he entered Jerusalem on that Palm Sunday.

Dressed in solid gold, he wore a crimson red cape that flowed out from behind him. There were thousands, yea, millions, billions of angels following him, all on snow white mounts- all fully equipped for battle.

My jaw dropped as I watched the angelic troops flying past, following their leader.

"Do you want to go?" Robert-el asked me.

"Are you kidding, I wouldn't miss it for the world."

Two white war horses appeared by my windows and we leaped on them and merged into the endless hosts of angels surging forward.

A colossal hole opened up before us and I saw Jesus and his army disappear down the huge black tunnel, changing from this dimensions back into that of space and time. There was no light at the end, only darkness- but our Lord sped onward, until beneath us we saw a blue marble against a black sky. Rapidly it increased in size until I recognized it as my old home planet, the Earth.

"YA-HOO!" I shouted as I plunged after my Leader.

"Hallelujah, it's the Second Coming of Christ."

TO BE CONTINUED

<u>SOON</u>

~*~ Revelation 19:11-14 ~*~

"Now I saw heaven opened, and behold, a white horse. And He who sat on him was called Faithful and True... and on His head were many crowns... He was clothed with a robe dipped in blood, and His name is called The Word of God. 14 And the armies in heaven, clothed in fine linen, white and clean, followed Him on white horses."

A Tribute to My Wonderful Wife, Sue

Sue Lenox Curlee was the kindest, most loving, most dedicated Christian I have ever known. Growing up poor, she won a scholarship to Judson College.

Because of friends and W.M.U., she attended the University of Alabama Medical School for two years-we were married and she was promised she could return when I finished Seminary.

The Mission Board would not appoint us, the administration of the school changed, babies came along, so she didn't finish her Medical Degree. But she never complained. She just raised our four children in the Christian Faith, encouraged me in the trials and tribulations of a pastor.
She was the perfect Pastor's Wife.

She returned to receive her Master's Degree in Special Education,
taught for 22 years, and loved every student

She was elected President of the Judson Alumni; named Alumna of the year; and served on the Board of Directors.

I have a better idea- Look her up in Heaven.
If you don't already, you will learn to love my wife.

Bob Curlee